RANDOM
HOUSE

LARGE
PRINT

THE Martha Rules

THE Martha

10 ESSENTIALS FOR ACHIEVING SUCCESS AS YOU START, BUILD, OR MANAGE A BUSINESS

Rules

Martha Stewart

RANDOM HOUSE
LARGE PRINT

Mention of specific companies, organizations, or authorities in this book does not imply endorsement by the publisher, nor does mention of specific companies, organizations, or authorities imply that they endorse this book.

Internet addresses and telephone numbers given in this book were accurate at the time it went to press.

© 2005 by Martha Stewart Living Omnimedia, Inc.

All rights reserved.
Published in the United States of America by Random House Large Print in association with Rodale, New York. Distributed by Random House, Inc., New York. No part of this publication may be reproduced or transmitted in any form or by any means, electronic or mechanical, including photocopying, recording, or any other information storage and retrieval system, without the written permission of the publisher.

Permission to reprint from **Entertaining,** by Martha Stewart, copyright © 1982, granted by Clarkson Potter, Random House, Inc.

Cover photograph © 2005 by Scott Duncan

Printed in the United States of America

The Library of Congress has established a Cataloging-in-Publication record for this title.

ISBN-13: 978-0-7393-2627-5
ISBN-10: 0-7393-2627-9

www.randomlargeprint.com

FIRST LARGE PRINT EDITION

10 9 8 7 6 5 4 3 2 1

This Large Print edition published in accord with the standards of the N.A.V.H.

I would like to dedicate this book to my
daughter, Alexis Stewart,
and all other young entrepreneurs
with hopes and dreams for a fine future.

Acknowledgments

There are many, many people who have inspired, taught, influenced, and supported me during the years that I have been visualizing, creating, building, and managing my own entrepreneurial venture. I want to thank every one of them for their efforts, energy, help, and advice. The construction of Martha Stewart Living Omnimedia has been a meaningful and exciting journey—not just for me, but for each and every colleague who has spent time with me, designing and erecting and maintaining a fine, worthwhile, productive American dream.

Contents

xii

Introduction

In 2004, I entered a federal prison camp in Alderson, West Virginia. There, amidst a thousand or so women, were hundreds of young, middle-aged, and older women who had dreams of starting a business when they were released. Many of them came to me to express their passion, their hopes, and their ideas. They were so like the myriad people who write to me with their ideas, seeking guidance, advice, hard facts, and a road map to a successful business.

Two very young women called me over to a picnic table one warm spring evening— there were metal picnic tables with benches at which we sat to talk, to plan, to read, and to eat the few "home-cooked" meals some of us concocted in the microwave ovens. Spread out before them were pages and pages of writing, drawings, calculations; this was their vision statement, their business plan, and the sketches of what their Big Idea would really look like once they were free to build their dream. I studied the plans. They wanted to create and operate a unisex hair salon combined with a café, salad bar, and soul food restaurant in a warehouse district of a large southern city.

Neither had much experience, neither was really a chef or a hairdresser, and neither had any experience running a business. I was astonished at the complexity of the idea, stunned at the expansiveness of the plan, and really pleased that two young dreamers wanted to set out on such an adventure. They were asking for advice, however, and I felt that as the experienced mentor, the entrepreneur with concrete success, I was required to be fair, circumspect, critical, and even blunt. I did not want to dampen their spirits; both still had a long while to spend confined in Alderson. So I wrote down the outline of this book and arranged to give a talk about starting a business, right there in the speakers' room, underneath the chapel. Using the young women's idea as an example, I spoke about dreams and passion and vision statements and business plans. I encouraged planning, investing, partnering, and careful, thoughtful research.

Expressing my concern that their plan was too ambitious, too expansive, too difficult, too expensive, and maybe even too old-fashioned, I explained that in New York and other metropolitan areas, hair salons were chic havens for beauty, health, personal care, and skin and nail care. Women did not want to eat where they had their hair cut—a fine cappuccino, maybe; a glass of iced tea and a sandwich on the run, okay. I encouraged them to divide the business in two: a restaurant, and a hair salon that catered to male and female customers. This was a better plan—the one-stop shopping plan that many retailers are now starting to develop. I told them which trade journals to read, what fashion magazines to study, and which books to gather to do their research.

When I returned home from Alderson, I had 5 months of home confinement, and I watched lots of late-night movies. One such movie was **Barbershop,** perhaps the inspiration for the young women's plan. I know that inspiration can be found in many different places. So did the girls.

Their Big Idea reminded me so much of a plan that I had proposed to a group of astute and experienced venture capitalists about 5 years ago, a group that had helped nurture and finance companies like Netscape, Google, Intuit, and many others. I was so enthusiastic about my idea, so talkative and effusive about its possibilities and its potentially wonderful impact on the world of homemakers. In return, I was stared at and discouraged with words and phrases such as, "It's too ambitious"; "It's too early for such an idea"; "It's too big"; "You're not focused." I used the criticisms and comments to reformulate the idea of Martha Stewart Living Omnimedia, and we are still working on it, still passionate about it.

Being an entrepreneur is not easy, but it is exciting, fun, and amazingly interesting and challenging. As you will read in the following chapters, being an entrepreneur requires a person to do more than just "go to work," much more than just "do a job." It requires eyes in the back of one's head; constant learning; curiosity; unflagging energy; good health, or at least a strong constitution that will ward off illnesses; and even the strength and desire to put up with sleep deprivation and long hours of intense concentration. To many, these characteristics might sound rather daunting, but among successful entrepreneurs, these are common traits.

The entrepreneurial spirit is alive and well. I see evidence of that fact each and every day. And because so many budding entrepreneurs have so many questions about how to take an idea and make it happen, I decided to write **The Martha Rules** as a practical and inspiring manual. My hope is that you will use it as a recipe book to make your own success.

THE Martha
Rules

What's passion got to do with it?

Martha's Rule

BUILD YOUR BUSINESS SUCCESS AROUND SOMETHING THAT YOU LOVE—SOMETHING THAT IS INHERENTLY AND ENDLESSLY INTERESTING TO YOU.

IT IS GREAT TO LOVE ONE'S WORK. Doing work that you enjoy gives you energy. You are imbued with enthusiasm. Your senses seem sharper. You wake up with new ideas every day and with solutions to conquer the challenges that cropped up the day before. You are always confident that goals are attainable, that creativity and ingenuity and hard work and passion for the work will make "it" all come together. This "passion" for one's work is just like an all-consuming love affair—something that all of us crave to experience but encounter only once or twice in a lifetime if we are lucky.

Knowing your passion, working hard to keep it alive, enjoying it every minute of every day, even when the going gets difficult—these are the hallmarks of an entrepreneurial enterprise that you build and develop and maintain and evolve. You expend this extraordinary energy so that others may benefit from it, may learn from it, and may even profit from it.

I have always found it extremely difficult to differentiate between what others might consider my life and my business. For me they are inextricably intertwined. That is because I have the same passion for both. Simply stated, my life is my work and my work is my life. As a result, I consider myself one of the lucky ones because I am excited every day: I love waking up; I love getting to work; I love focusing on a new initiative.

I am not alone with this passion for my

work, for my life. Other entrepreneurs that I know have the same type of passion, and their excitement for their work and for their lives is electric and palpable. Whether they work for a large company, run their own business, are raising a family, or are organizing a fund-raising event for a charity, they are tuned into anything and anyone that can help them make their plans unfold and their dreams come true. They are positive and optimistic. They always find a way to get the job done better, faster, and more energetically than those around them.

Passion is the first and most essential ingredient for planning and beginning a business or for starting and satisfactorily completing any worthwhile project. Without passion, work is just work, a chore. Without passion, quality, the cornerstone of all businesses, is simply about minimum standards. Without passion, the people who will benefit directly from your efforts—the customers—seem incidental.

It was my passion for teaching and for easing the challenges of the homemaker's everyday life that helped me turn my homegrown catering business into a successful omnime-dia company with hundreds of millions of dollars in revenue, and with hundreds of similarly creative and driven employees de-signing and producing thousands of exciting and useful products for America's home-makers.

When work is based in passion, it does not feel like work—it feels fulfilling and em-powering, far more about creating, building, devising, initiating, leading, and serving than about simply moving through one task and on to another. I often use the following example: For me, planting and maintaining a garden is not, is **never,** working in the gar-den. Instead, it is gardening. I never have to do housework. I have furniture to polish, I have vacuuming to do, I have ironing to finish.

Search until you find your passion

You may already know your life's calling as surely as you know your eye color or your favorite flavor of ice cream. Perhaps you have envisioned yourself running your own ski school or designing a line of fine paper products for so long it already seems real. You are just trying to find out how to get going, how to transform your dream into a business.

Or you may feel a burning desire to start **something** and run **something,** but you are not sure what that something is. Business schools are filled with people who feel this way, people putting together the tools to hit the ground running as soon as they figure out where they want to go.

Or perhaps most commonly, you may find yourself in a situation where you feel vaguely restless. You may have a perfectly good job, but you feel an urge, a tugging, a preoccupation with an idea. You are turning it over in your mind like a Rubik's Cube, rehearsing how you are going to tell your family and friends about "it" in serious, measured tones. You are preoccupied with trying to figure out how you can make money with "it" so people will not think you have lost all sense. But the private notion you keep coming back to is: "How fun this could be!"

When I look back on the years when I was exploring career choices and discovering my true entrepreneurial spirit, my choices seem rather eclectic. I was barely in my teens when I began taking a bus from my home in Nutley, New Jersey, to New York City, where I worked as a photographer's model. I was the envy of my girlfriends, making much better wages for a few hours' work than they did babysitting or doing chores. This work was fun and lucrative. It demanded a certain optimism and a drive that not everyone possesses.

In the freelance world, you start every day at zero. There are no guarantees of future or regular income. This freelance life taught me to believe in myself and work hard and that good things (and income) would come of it as a result. However, by the time I married and finished my college studies in history and architectural history, I was tired of the modeling business. Modeling was a wonderful way to supplement our family's income, but I wanted to build a career. I longed to do something more intellectually stimulating.

Armed mainly with my father's encouragement that I could do anything I put my mind to, I considered my options. I had no capital to start my own business. I did, however, have a great desire to work hard and learn. So I went to Wall Street and joined a small brokerage house where I learned how to be a stockbroker, buying and selling stocks; and I watched closely as many companies' fortunes rose and fell. I saw some companies make terrible blunders and others, such as McDonald's and Electronic Data Systems, grow and grow. It was an outstanding education in business and often was very exciting, but I never developed a passion for the brokerage business.

When we (my husband, our baby, and I) moved to Connecticut, I decided to leave Wall Street and try something different. I loved houses and landscaping and decorating, so I thought real estate might be a good career for me. I studied and eventually got my real estate license, but I soon realized that the actual work of selling houses involved spending many hours driving around with clients. That was not something that I wanted to do. I left the business without ever hosting an open house or selling a single property!

I tell you all this because it is not uncommon to try a number of different things before your passion becomes clear. Experimentation is the only way to figure it out. By trying out different businesses and jobs that interest you, you will learn things that will later help you. For example, when I quit modeling, I never imagined I would again spend so much time in front of still and television cameras, and yet I did and still do, regularly. As a stockbroker, I watched many companies take on too much debt and expand too rapidly. It made me vow never to build a business on debt. I also saw companies in which dynamic leaders inspired employees to attain impressive goals—and so I've worked hard to motivate people and hire the right executives.

Even my brief time in real estate held an important lesson. Although I disliked driving clients around, looking at houses with them, I loved looking at real estate as an investment for myself. I discovered that the true work of a given job may be much different than what you imagine. There may be a public face to certain businesses that seems fun, exciting, even glamorous. The backroom realities may be another story altogether.

The restaurant business is like this. Running a restaurant is only partly about cooking delectable dishes and greeting regular, friendly customers at the door with a big, welcoming smile. You have to know how to buy foods of appropriate quality and quantity. You need to understand the culinary needs and wants of the community in which your restaurant is located. You must hire and manage kitchen workers and a wait staff. You have to be prepared to fill in as a carpenter, plumber, bartender, dishwasher, or locksmith if that is what it takes on any given day to keep the doors open. On top of those challenges, the hours are terrible, and you will never spend a holiday with your family. Considering all of these obstacles, it is a miracle there are so many great restaurants.

Try new things. I promise that no matter what you experience, you will learn lessons that will eventually help you choose a business you love and a job you will cherish.

Catering paved the way

Even before I found my entrepreneurial spirit, one thing I did know was that I enjoyed cooking and focusing on the home. I loved experimenting in the kitchen. I began baking pies and selling them at a local market. I opened a small gourmet food market called the Marketbasket within a fabulous clothing store that specialized in Ralph Lauren fashions. I sold my own foodstuffs as well as those I commissioned from local women who had a passion for cooking and baking but no desire to run a business, as I did. Clients came in droves to buy scones, quiches, birthday cakes, and Sunday dinners.

Then I took a bigger step: I started a catering business, The Uncatered Affair, in a small kitchen in my Turkey Hill home. The kitchen was a far cry from the spacious and airy kitchens of my homes today, which are equipped with the latest commercial-grade appliances, right down to the San Marco espresso/cappuccino machines. My Turkey Hill kitchen was located in the basement and shared space with the laundry room. The thick, early-19th-century stone walls kept the room cool, and there was no heat—just the warmth that came from my one small commercial stove with two ovens. But that helped cut down on my need for refrigeration (which was good, because I had only one refrigerator), and there were lots and lots of butcher-block countertops on which to work.

I must admit that I did not exactly start small. My first catering job was a wedding for more than 300 people. I charged only $12 per person for the food. I served the guests a spectacular meal of hors d'oeuvres, oeufs en gelée, stuffed chicken breast, pâtés, pyramids of white peaches, two wedding cakes, and ice creams. Here is what I wrote about this wedding in my first book, **Entertaining:**

The menu was a novice's—extravagant, demanding, and unprofitable:

hors d'oeuvres, homemade pâtés, cold cucumber soup, salmon mousses, cold bass, chicken breast chaud-froid, and homemade breads. Down on Long Island Sound, on a sweltering August afternoon in an unsheltered beach club in Darien, I stood by the buffet table and watched the aspic melt off the oeufs en gelée, and the top tier of a basketweave cake slip starboard. I eliminated the oeufs and pushed the cake back in place. Nevertheless, it was a very good party, and I knew I was hooked. That first party was important, because I learned a lot of small things: that a tent in an atrium stifles any breeze; that fans can be rented; and that no one will know about your disasters if you don't tell him. In a larger sense, I learned how good spirits and optimism can carry the day.

From that first event I knew immediately that I had found an enterprise that combined several of my talents, my interests, and some of my business experience.

I realized that successful caterers provided good service and delicious, substantial food. I vowed to do even more—to go from good to great. I catered events with flair, originality, and a sense of style. I worked incredibly hard to set myself apart from other caterers. My parties had to look different, they had to taste different, and they had to deliver an altogether different experience than those of other caterers. Nothing was too much effort. I would stay up all night reading recipe books and researching festive motifs for parties before I would prepare a proposal. I did not approach any project with ease or abandon, and there was no amount of research into any aspect of what I was doing that I considered excessive or not worth the effort. My reputation began to grow, and I began getting referrals to more and more customers. The local newspapers took notice, and my fledgling business was profiled on the front pages of the **Westport News** and the **Fairpress,** both in Connecticut.

More important, customers soon realized that they could trust my advice. I had reasons for what I was recommending, and I could explain them. If I did not know the answer to a question, I would track it down. I paid attention and learned everything I could to help my business. I listened to what my customers wanted, and I thought about things that would help me do my job better.

Catering paved the way for me to find my true passion as a teacher and a communicator of Good Things. To me, Good Things mean simple, practical solutions or tips that make everyday activities easier. The first time I used the expression publicly was later, on my television show. I was being filmed in the garden, and I held up my garden trowel, which had a brightly painted orange handle so it wouldn't get lost among the greenery. "It's a good thing," I said.

Write the book you want to read

Although I hadn't yet "coined" the term when I ran my catering business, I already had a great deal of experience developing Good Things: ways to make my own catering projects easier and more efficient. And I intuitively knew that entertaining well was not simply a performance, but an expression of important human emotions: joy, gratitude, love, generosity, and friendship, to name only a few. I could see that my catering clients wished they had specific resources to help them think about all the different elements of entertaining. Frankly, at times I wished I had such a resource, which led to my first Big Idea. There were cookbooks, there were decorating books, there were flower-arranging books, and there were etiquette books. Why not combine all those elements into one beautiful book based on the concept of entertaining?

Many caterers might have smiled like Mona Lisa when their clients asked them questions, worrying that if everyone learned to do these things themselves, what would be left to cater? Instead, I went from thinking of myself as a caterer, which was an enjoyable and satisfying but extremely difficult job, to making myself an expert on entertaining. This was a far more interesting, expansive, and exciting notion—one that filled me with so many ideas I could barely sleep. That is how I came to author **Entertaining.**

There were plenty of doubters. There had never been a book like it, some publishers complained. (Exactly, I said.) I was convinced that the passion and experience I could bring to the project and the great need for a book addressing that subject would make it a best-seller.

Entertaining went on to sell more than a million copies and launched the most important phase of my career. I discovered that I loved teaching people to do the things that I enjoyed doing, and I loved encouraging people to do them well. **Entertaining** also served as my first introduction to the notion of synergy, a powerful business concept that refers to the value created when you combine similar or diverse elements in an intelligent way. At this early phase of my career, I took 300 excellent, tried-and-true recipes, extraordinarily colorful illustrative photography, and tasteful advice on party giving and menu planning, and put them together in a beautiful, informative book that actually helped many, many people discover their own love and talent for entertaining and cooking and that helped transform the cookbook genre in the process.

The journey begins in the mirror

If you want to begin the journey to discover your entrepreneurial passion, you first must analyze your own interests, strengths, weaknesses, and desires. You must consider carefully how hard you want to work. And then you must research **in a serious way** the job or field in which you believe you might want to work.

DAN HINKLEY
A passion for plants

My longtime friend, the extraordinary plant horticulturist and entrepreneur Dan Hinkley, used to observe his father working nights and weekends at his family's drugstore in the Midwest. He recalls resenting the time his father had to spend at work. As Dan grew older, however, he realized that he too had a business idea that was important to him: He loved studying and working with exotic plants, and he dreamed of opening his own nursery.

Dan is the sort of frugal, patient entrepreneur that I am, and he was not about to go into debt. So he started his business slowly, happy in the early years that his small nursery could help finance his plant-hunting travels by making them tax-deductible. If you take the adventures of the famous orchid thief from Susan Orlean's best-selling book of that name and multiply them by 50, you will begin to understand the exciting adventures that Dan has enjoyed traveling up and down mountains and trekking through the world's forests and plains in search of unknown, undiscovered, unique, and uncataloged exotic plants.

As his reputation and his stock grew, Dan's exquisite Heronswood Nursery and experimental garden near Seattle became well known among serious plant people. He began lecturing to garden groups and in schools, making guest appearances on television shows like mine, and writing books. Pretty soon, he was working the same kind of hours his father used to work in his store. But, like most happy entrepreneurs, he admitted there was nothing he would have rather done.

Today, Heronswood is a well-known and respected nursery business. Although it was purchased for an impressive sum by the large seed company, Burpee, several years ago, Dan still runs it. Dan remains just as infatuated with his subject matter today. "There is no faking passion; you either have it or you don't. If you have it, go for it." He has discovered hundreds of previously elusive species of plants, flowers, and shrubs and made them available in this country before anyone else. As a very good businessman, Dan has used technology to build his reputation as well as his customer base. A visit to the Heronswood

Web site reveals fantastic explanations and descriptions for his plants:

Asplenium scolopendrium . . . From a durable evergreen species known as the Hart's Tongue Fern, this sensational cultivar possesses a thrilly frilly leaf margin, creating a rippling rosette and sensational groundcover or specimen in shaded situations. Drought tolerant once fully established, this is a widespread species that I have enjoyed in both the woodlots of England as well as the mountains of N. Japan.

Doesn't this make you want a thrilly frilly fern for your shady situations? Dan is a man who has combined his heart's desire with a unique, successful business. A classic entrepreneur.

Become an apprentice

There is an energy and enthusiasm that defines Dan. He, like other successful entrepreneurs, is so passionate about his work that he attracts people to him who can help him succeed. I enjoyed having Dan on my television program; he has provided fascinating information to my viewers. For Dan, appearing on the show helped increase the public's awareness of his nursery. As a result, enthusiastic young horticulturalists want to work for him. Just as when Dan was starting out and mentors were happy to help him, Dan's success has inspired a new generation of apprentices.

When you are truly committed to your goals, curious to learn, and eager to work hard, great mentors will be pleased to share what they know. I think of mentors in a broad sense. The late Julia Child, for example, was a generous and important mentor to me, although I did not get to know her personally until I already was a published author. I had devoured her cookbooks long before I met her; I taught myself the art of French cuisine by systematically preparing every single one of her recipes in volumes one and two of **Mastering the Art of French Cooking.** I personally mastered the classics of French cuisine—pâte feuilletée, baguettes, crème anglaise, coq au vin—from the pages of her books, and those recipes became the basis for my deep interest in all good food and recipes from around the world. I found that I could truly consider her a mentor, a teacher, a guide, even though I did not talk to her, because she reached me clearly and thoroughly through her excellent recipes and instructions.

In my lifelong love affair with gardening, I have had many mentors. My first was my father, who loved growing tomatoes and other wonderful fresh vegetables and flowers in the two-level garden that he built in our backyard. As his apprentice—I started when I was about 3—I was charged with removing weeds from the cracks in the cobblestone path with a flathead screwdriver. Sometime later I discovered a book called **A Woman's Hardy Garden** by Helena Rutherfurd Ely. I meticulously studied the text and its instructions, experimenting with informal flower border styles and Mrs. Ely's ingenious, if eccentric, gardening techniques. (She would save or discard plants by utilizing an elaborate system of color-coded ribbons, tying them around plants to mark them for extracting seeds or cuttings.)

As my interests in gardening became more and more sophisticated, I collected many more wonderful mentors. To this day, I keep lists of gardens, gardeners, and nurseries all over the world that I would like to visit or that I have visited, so that, when I travel and find myself with some free time, I can learn about new garden designs, discuss new growing techniques, or collect unusual specimens for my own gardens. I have spent countless hours "harvesting" information from dozens of plantsmen, and I find those generous gardeners almost unfailingly happy to answer as many questions as I can pose.

In my business life, I have met many brilliant entrepreneurs from whom I have collected many ideas and new perspectives. The first time I met Rupert Murdoch was in 1989, when I was presenting News Corp. with my idea for a new magazine. The meeting was good, but it became great when he walked in. Here was a very charismatic businessman who had built a media empire the likes of which people hadn't seen before. I was awestruck at the atmospheric change that occurred in the office when he bolted into the room, strong and vital and powerful.

Another deservedly famous and brilliant businessman is Warren Buffett, the "sage of Omaha." More than anything, I value Mr. Buffett's commonsense outlook and fundamental frugality. (The license plate on his car reads "Thrifty.") He is famous for taking a felt pen and yellow pad and hand-writing his annual report to shareholders of his company, Berkshire Hathaway. His wisdom on investing and managing diverse businesses in complicated times ranks Warren's ideas and opinions and philosophy high among any you will hear from the hallowed halls of an Ivy League business school. He has served as an inspiration to so many businesspeople, from the late Katharine Graham, to Microsoft's founder, Bill Gates.

Learn all you can from your mentors. Try to work alongside them. Their passion will amplify your passion. The concept of an apprentice is an ancient and wise one, and if you can find such a position early in your career and have the chance to work with a master, take it! The enthusiasm, deep under-standing, and endless curiosity of a true ex-pert will infect you, whether you are simply trying to reinforce your own knowledge about a hobby or interest, or whether you are figuring out the kind of entrepreneur you want to become.

When you love what you do, it's not work

I hope I have made it clear that your entre-preneurial mentor may not necessarily come from your own field. I have had the pleasure of acting as a mentor to a number of suc-cessful entrepreneurs. One of them is the chic and sophisticated New York hair and makeup stylist Eva Scrivo.

EVA SCRIVO
Caring about her customers

From the first time Eva cut and styled my hair nearly 10 years ago, it was obvious to me that she was a premier hair stylist and a gifted makeup artist.

When I met Eva, I was intrigued by her exotic good looks, her careful and studied approach to her craft, and her deep-seated confidence in her talent. Her confidence comes from a thorough understanding of the techniques of her craft, but she also has a sense of people and personality and style that has brought a long list of prominent women to her salon, including Senator Hillary Rodham Clinton, Aretha Franklin, Fran Drescher, and Lauren Hutton.

It did not take many sessions of what has become a very close association— literally nose-to-nose when she is applying my makeup—for me to see that Eva is not simply a hairdresser or makeup person; she is a gifted entrepreneur.

Eva is a person who did recognize her calling early in life. Ever since she was a young girl, she dreamed of becoming a famous New York stylist. Her entrepreneurial drive appeared early as well. Eva's first success in business came at age 13, when she went to her father's antique store after school to do her homework and ended up single-handedly selling one of the most expensive pieces in the store. When her father offered to give her $50 as a commission, she politely and firmly demanded the 10 percent ($400!) commission that she knew the other salesmen made!

When I am getting ready for television and photo shoots, I am not the sort to chitchat about the weather. Eva and I would much rather talk about the design and content of the show. It has even been my pleasure over the years to talk with Eva about her ideas for expanding her business. She has told me that I inspired her to expand her business from a small, three-seat shop in the East Village to a very much larger, full-service salon in the West Village. She has become a full-fledged entrepreneur.

If you had been sitting near us while she styled my hair, you might have thought I sounded more like a naysayer than a supporter. We have talked about everything from real estate rentals to the kinds of amenities a high-end spa should offer. We have talked about managing employees and about leases and contracts. I grilled her with the kind of questions I have already mentioned: What exactly are you trying to accomplish? Are you sure the market will support what you are trying to do? Will you be able to get the right help and provide the level of service you personally offer as you expand? Can you afford the rent on a large space? Can you market your talents?

Eva could have had a long and very profitable career just tending to her private clients out of the small shop she used to have on Seventh Street. Because Eva listens so carefully to her clients, however, she began to recognize a need. She often heard clients complain about the service and attitudes they perceived in many of New York's high-end spas and salons. As Eva explains it, "So many things in my industry are poorly executed, from the comfort and design of the salon facilities, to the aloof manner of salon and spa personnel, to the quality of products salons sell."

As you can see, Eva is a woman who pays attention. She does not look around her and simply copy the competition; she thinks deeply about how customers **should** be treated. As we talked, it was clear that the salons that Eva's clients were complaining about had violated another of my rules for business: They were not providing a quality experience. They might have had talented employees and good products, but customers did not feel well taken care of. The atmosphere was not welcoming and comfortable. Eva was smart enough to realize that that quality gap created an opportunity for what I call a Big Idea. As you will learn in the next chapter, I never judge an idea for a business solely by whether it is unique or unusual. I judge it by whether it addresses a genuine customer need and by whether it will be a superior alternative to their other options.

Two years ago, Eva and her husband decided to open their own, much bigger salon that featured an array of spa services in addition to hair styling and skin care. They had an opportunity to obtain a reasonable lease in what is now one of New York's most expensive and desirable commercial areas—the Meatpacking District. They opened a large, chic, elegant salon, which is doing very, very well. Eva now employs 30 people and continues to style a most impressive client list. She offers massage and acupuncture services. She carries a line of outstanding beauty products. She is developing her own private label products. She is on every beauty magazine's list of the hottest stylists, and her salon is frequently mentioned as among the city's best. Her philosophy is to make sure every customer feels like she is monitoring his or her experience personally, an attitude that extends to specific details such as serving lovely, herbal teas and providing comfortable ottomans for the customer's feet in the shampoo stations. Eva says, "I try to pour a little bit of my own diva-ness into understanding what my customers like and want. When you love what you do, it's not work."

Becoming a first-rate entrepreneur begins with loving your work and becoming expert in it, and I believe this thriving salon is only the beginning for Eva Scrivo. What has always impressed me is how careful and serious Eva is about her business and about her customers. She really cares about how they look and feel not only while they are in the salon but when they leave.

You will find that when you have a passion for what you do, and if you are sincere about your interest and concern for your customers, then "work" becomes a genuine pleasure.

Do not confuse enthusiasm for passion

Like many smart entrepreneurs, Eva developed a deep knowledge about the fundamentals of her businesses before she expanded. She paid her dues working in other shops, and she picked up valuable information that informed her subsequent plans and ideas. I agree with Eva when she points out that there is more to becoming an entrepreneur than being an expert. "There are a lot more experts than there are successful entrepreneurs," she notes. However, courage and enthusiasm also are insufficient.

I am troubled when I hear about otherwise intelligent people who have made the mistake of risking their hard-earned savings or leaving a good job to pursue a brand-new venture about which they know almost nothing. They become enamored with an idea and talk only to people who will encourage them uncritically, instead of seeking out mentors or advisors who will objectively analyze their idea. This is natural, but it is actually heartbreaking to see smart, capable people rush into a situation without the proper preparation or research.

At the earliest stages of a venture, sometimes entrepreneurs get their priorities mixed up. They mistake enthusiasm and impatience for the more basic passion that inspires people to want to learn and become expert and make good decisions. Dan Hinkley used to teach a class at a community college on running a plant nursery. His students often were people who were considering a career change and wanted to open their own nurseries. "I would always tell them that your biggest investment for the first 3 years should be a wheelbarrow and a shovel," he says in his understated, wry style. Spending lots of money "is a real seduction to people who think they can't even get started before they buy a big truck and a backhoe and all kinds of equipment. The truth is, what you need to learn about this business is how much hard work it is. You have to discover whether you really love the work and you are able to do the physical labor. I got a good piece of advice from my dad about trying things: 'If you can't keep up, how are you going to catch up?'"

There are situations where someone has an idea so unusual or original that there is no good model for how to go about developing it. The only option in that case is to just jump in with both feet. I can think of

several very well-known, successful entrepreneurs who did this, including some of
the best-known high-technology executives
in the country: Steve Jobs of Apple Computer, Larry Ellison of Oracle, and, of
course, Bill Gates of Microsoft.

Bill Gates was a freshman at Harvard
when he found himself so passionately interested in computers and software that he
could not imagine waiting to finish college
before launching his own company. He
dropped out to pursue his ideas and created
one of the most valuable companies in the
world, Microsoft, which creates and sells
products used by millions and millions of
people. He was just a kid, but there was no
internship program or work experience that
could have taught him how to start and
grow a software company that had set its
sights on making computers useful to vast
numbers of companies and individuals. He
was truly at the cutting edge because he
had technical expertise as well as a novel
Big Idea.

That sort of situation is very rare, however. It is also important to realize that Bill

was an extremely bright young man, and for him, dropping out of school to do this was not the sort of risk it might be for most people. His father was a sophisticated businessperson, and Bill had been exposed to basic business principles. If this venture had not worked out, he would have had plenty of opportunities to return to school and follow a more traditional route. The success stories with these sorts of origins are quite unique. Most have emerged in the short window following a scientific breakthrough that opened the door for innovation—in manufacturing, communications, transportation, or, in the case of Bill Gates, technology. My point is that it is fine to look at Bill Gates as a model of drive, determination, and intelligence, but please do not simply abandon your education or current job with the misplaced faith that your enthusiasm will be enough for success.

Another entrepreneur whose intensity, curiosity, research, and devotion to quality impress me is a gentleman who first flagged me down on an East Hampton back road several years ago. I had decided to go for a ride on my turquoise Velocifero scooter and was zipping along when I heard a shout: "Yo, Martha!" Across the street on his own turquoise scooter was Sean "Diddy" Combs, the rap star who used to be called Puff Daddy and then P. Diddy.

Sean has had his share of high-profile adventures and misadventures. You probably see him as a tough guy who would be the last person interested in Martha Stewart's list of Good Things. You would be wrong about that. Sean has done well for himself. As the CEO and chairman of Bad Boy Worldwide Entertainment Group, he made **Fortune** magazine's list of the most influential minorities in business in 2005, and he is interested in doing things in a high-quality way. Sean and I have had several conversations about mass marketing and how to position high-quality products. He is a very serious man, and he shares my curiosity in trying to learn everything he can about the ventures in which he is involved. I cheered when he ran the New York Marathon, because he wanted to do something that involved intensive training and that showed that he was not just a celebrity, but also a hard-working, determined individual.

Ultimately, businesspeople who do well have more in common than may be obvious from the type of product they sell or their personal style. They have passion, curiosity, a work-hard ethic, and a commitment to doing what they do with the highest degree of excellence.

Challenging, satisfying work gives you energy

The delightful secret of the entrepreneurial life is that when you love your work, you rarely get tired. You are so driven to do what you do well, that every piece of knowledge or insight you work to develop acts like fuel: It gives you momentum. Think about some of the great entrepreneurs you have heard about. You would never read that Larry Ellison of Oracle said he was tired. J. K. Rowling, the author of the marvelous Harry Potter series, did not stop writing after her first best-seller because these 600-plus-page opuses were just too much work. Fred Smith of Federal Express revolutionized the delivery business by convincing every employee to go above and beyond the basics to make sure that every single customer received exceptional service every day. Imagine if he had been intimidated by just how much effort all that would be.

I was thinking about hard work and passion the other day when I was watching those crazed "iron chefs" on television. Each one is an incredibly gifted and creative chef. They do not need to compete on television; they do not need to cook complicated, impromptu meals using exotic ingredients, with no recipes and no planning. However, they are consumed with passion for what they love to do, and they love to demonstrate their expertise and their ability to think on their feet. They are willing to risk respect and reputation as they scramble to create and compete.

That is passion on display.

Ask yourself,
What's the Big Idea?

Martha's Rule

2

FOCUS YOUR ATTENTION AND CREATIVITY
ON BASIC THINGS, THINGS THAT PEOPLE
NEED AND WANT. THEN LOOK FOR WAYS
TO ENLARGE, IMPROVE, AND ENHANCE
YOUR BIG IDEA.

PASSION CAN BE A WILD THING, taking
you in many directions. Try to grab it by
the reins and, as you harness that passion to
start or grow your business, begin to focus
on a goal. It is important to think about
your business ideas in a clear and disci-
plined way, tuning in to precisely what it is

that your customers need and want; then concentrate on thinking big.

Looking back on my journey as an entrepreneur, it is quite clear, to me at least, that everything I have ever done has stemmed from a desire to provide as many people as possible with products and services that they absolutely need and absolutely want. Because my work is primarily about domestic arts, this has been a relatively easy task; I consider myself to be a part of my broad and ever-growing audience, so this "zeroing in" has been more focused and more exact than if I were the inventor of a new gadget or electronic tool. Homemaking, homekeeping, has been a topic of enormous interest to me, and I really can and do determine what my customers need and want by what I need and want, whether it is a delicious new recipe, a functional and useful garden tool, a memorable way to celebrate a traditional holiday, a unique way to redecorate a room, or a different approach to landscaping a backyard.

My advice to you as an entrepreneur? Take off your shoes and step into your customers' shoes for a while. Take a walk down their street and ask yourself, "Is there a use for my idea in her life?" Or, in my case, "Would the colors that I love on this paint chart really look good in his house?" "Would a digest-size magazine of easy-to-follow recipes called **Everyday Food** be useful to this family?"

Thomas Edison, one of the most prolific inventors of all time, may have seemed a bit eccentric with all his tinkering of unusual objects. But even he stated, "I have never perfected an invention that I did not think about in terms of the service it might give to others. . . . I find out what the world needs, and then I proceed to invent." And just look what he gave the world—the lightbulb, the phonograph, and even an improved-upon version of Alexander Graham Bell's newfangled telephone!

Out of frustration often comes a good idea

When you are alert and tuned in to the world around you, it is interesting to note how often your personal frustration can help you experience a Big Idea. My own brand of paint in all of my favorite colors was created just this way. The world around us is filled with seemingly endless rainbows of color. I have often observed how natural objects can blend together with perfect balance of tone and subtlety. Years ago, I was preparing to re-decorate several rooms in my home, and when I went to the paint store to choose colors, the natural hues that I longed for just were not available at the time. It suddenly became quite clear to me that I would have to formulate my own paint colors, borrowing them from nature, so the palette I wanted—needed—would be attainable.

What a fun and exciting project for me and my employees. We started with the eggs from my mix of rare and exotic chickens. In addition to the delicate whites, rich creams, and subtle beiges of some of the shells, my Araucana hens' eggs came in gorgeous shades of pale blue and green. I did not see those colors on the charts or in the selections found in my local paint store. Inspired, I also studied the myriad hues on a large, lovely seashell, mottled with soft browns and pinkish corals. Then I gathered leaves and bark and stones and dissected them, separating each of the many colors found on those objects. Many wonderful tones were discovered in the fur of my eight cats and the hairy coats of my Chow Chows. I don't think I had ever looked at the world in such a way before. We soon had 600 ideas for new colors.

We needed a partner to manufacture paints in these new colors and settled on Sherwin-Williams because of their high-quality products and huge customer base. My favorite part to this story is that Sherwin-Williams initially told us that their computers contained every color imaginable and that matching my shades would be very easy. But when we brought them our 600 samples, their computers could match only 10 or so! So far there are 416 distinctive hues of paint in the Martha Stewart Signature Color Palette, and 39 color combinations that are precoordinated across the entire Martha Stewart Signature line of home furnishings. So you can see, you should never accept what is offered to you if you feel it can be improved. There are many gaps and voids, many unmet needs in our complex world.

Dr. Brent Ridge, an assistant professor and geriatric medicine specialist at Mount Sinai School of Medicine in New York City, is focusing on one such void. I admire Dr. Ridge's Big Idea because, like Edison, he is looking to help and serve his customers. He came up with an exciting idea based on a simple but potentially huge business proposition: that the time was right to overhaul how hearing devices were sold in this country. Hearing loss is tragic and very sad to witness as it occurs. Once common only in old age, it is happening with greater frequency among the aging baby boomers. No one likes to admit that their hearing is going, but hearing-aid technology has improved to the point that the new, tiny devices are nearly invisible, easy to use, and not embarrassing. However, they can be quite costly—upwards of $5,000 for a pair with tests and fittings.

What Dr. Ridge is determined to do is to reinvent the business of selling hearing aids by launching a chain of stores that will be stylish and inviting, with a sleek, modern appeal consistent with the slender profile of today's hearing aids. Dr. Ridge not only understands the technology and science of hearing problems, he is also sensitive to the human side of business, including the psychology of resistance. He senses that people will feel more inclined to spend the money if they can have a similar kind of experience in his stores as they do when they purchase high-tech electronic equipment or some other high-value product. Dr. Ridge is poised to turn a problem into what I believe will be a very smart and successful business venture. Perhaps as he succeeds and sells more and more hearing aids, the prices will come down to be more in line with most peoples' pocketbooks. Witness what has occurred in the eyeglass industry: Prices have fallen over the years, and many of us now have several stylish pairs of glasses, with various tintings and fancier frames.

Revolutionizing the hearing-aid business is a wonderful idea with great potential, but I also want you to realize that there are many good Big Ideas that are more modest in their aims and don't demand a full-time commitment. One such idea was developed in the 1950s by Bette Nesmith Graham, an efficient, skilled Dallas secretary, who took great pride in her work. When she occasionally made a mistake on her typewriter and needed to correct it, she was unhappy with the eraser marks. Bette, who was also an artist, went home and began experimenting with her kitchen blender, mixing tempera paints to match the color of the paper she was using at work. She took a small bottle of the liquid to her job and found that, with careful application, typing mistakes were virtually unnoticeable. Her fellow secretaries were impressed and always asked to borrow her Mistake Out, as she initially called it. It was such a popular item that she went on to start her own business selling what became the very successful product known as Liquid Paper.

I mention this story because I actually know a modern-day Bette Graham—my talented and meticulous manicurist, Deborah Lippmann. Just as I was dissatisfied with the choice of paint colors offered to me, Deborah wasn't happy with the colors and quality of nail polishes on the market. Working with a chemist, she started mixing enamels—like Bette in her kitchen—and she did, indeed, come up with a superior formula. About 5 years ago, she proudly launched the Lippmann Collection. Deborah is also a wonderful jazz singer, and she wanted to give this nail polish line a little of her own personal pizzazz, so she tapped her favorite jazz songs for names like "Makin' Whoopee" and "Sophisticated Lady." Word of this quality nail polish spread quickly to Deborah's many celebrity clients, and now she is selling both polish and hand care products at Bergdorf Goodman, Sephora, Neiman Marcus, Nordstrom, and Henri Bendel.

Enough ideas for 100 Julys

As you compile your list of ideas for starting or growing a business and begin researching which ones are most viable, it is important but also great fun to brainstorm, bringing forth as many ideas as possible. I think about new concepts constantly, with or without another person or team. I greatly prefer thinking out loud with a team, however, and like any good, productive think-tank leader, I try to seek out and surround myself with people who just percolate fresh, original, and creative ideas. Sometimes, a small group of us will take just a single idea—a cover story for the magazine on home renovation, for example—and we will brainstorm different approaches for each element of the story, from how the story will start to what kind of photography will best illustrate it. Other times, I will ask each of my television producers to come up with 10 ideas for segments on a particular topic, such as gardening. I have 15 producers, so that's 150 ideas! We discuss the merits of each idea, one by one. And I try to move the discussion along as quickly as possible because the more you get people to think about why ideas are good or bad, the more fabulous are the ideas that result.

My very busy editors at **Martha Stewart Living** magazine are prime examples of the kinds of employees an entrepreneur needs and wants. Our editors collaborate with our photographers so that the written text will blend perfectly with the gorgeous photographs. Art directors choose just the right type style, and copy editors match that with an informative and clever headline and meaningful text. My Big Idea was to make sure that each issue is an appealing and informative mix of how-to information and inspiring ideas, dealing with decorating, cooking, gardening, homekeeping, celebrating, pet-keeping, collecting, and entertaining. My colleagues do their jobs extremely well, and I can assure you that it is not easy work. However, they love what they do, and they are proud of the result. And with all the brainstorming that goes on, we never run out of new ideas.

The very first issue of my magazine appeared on newsstands almost 15 years ago, but I still recall vividly compiling the prototype to attract investors. We decided on a July theme and chose appropriate photographs and recipes for a midsummer issue. We took it to a very serious magazine publishing house, where I met with the president of the firm. I was rather stunned by his reaction. After thumbing through the pages, he said, "Well, this is fine, but what are you going to do next July?" Clearly, he lacked imagination and understanding of the subject matter. Laughing, I said, "Oh, we have thousands of ideas relating to the Fourth of July." Fifteen years later, we are still going strong; and believe me, my editors and I probably have enough ideas for at least 100 more Julys!

Different is not always better

As a businessperson and as a person who gives high marks for creativity, I must say that I often see no inherent value in something simply because it is different. For example, sweeping sums of money have been made throughout history by people who sell commodities: staples like wheat, pork bellies, oil, or copper. There is no new or unique way to spur demand for these items, but impeccable timing in buying and selling is the Big Idea that makes investing in commodities profitable.

Another Big Idea that adds value to a product without changing it is Domino's Pizza. Domino's did not invent the pizza pie; the company simply rethought the pizza-delivery business on a large scale, thereby improving the customer experience. Domino's came up with a reliable way for large numbers of customers to order pizza by telephone and have it delivered quickly to their doors.

So unless you sense that your customers envision something different as something better, it does not pay **just** to be different.

Bake the cake that people
most want to eat

Back when my everyday business was catering, one of my signature offerings was my wedding cakes. Many bakers shy away from the stressful task of constructing and delivering wedding cakes, but I actually enjoy the challenge. One must be part chemist, part engineer, part architect, part artist—and all baker and pastry chef! The cake must look beautiful, taste extraordinary, and generously feed all the guests at the wedding. One must also transport the cake—an extremely difficult and tricky maneuver for something so large, intricate, and delicate. I was particularly interested, then, to see one of my favorite catering tasks presented to the teams competing on one of the episodes of my television show **The Apprentice: Martha Stewart.**

I told the teams to design, create, and deliver a wedding cake for display at a wedding fair held in a Michael C. Fina store. The purpose of the assignment was to entice actual customers into ordering a cake for a future wedding. The cakes had to be sold "as is." One team designed and produced a traditional multilayered, cream-colored cake. The other team created a cake that was very distinctive: asymmetrical and pink. I was very curious to see which design would win out. After all, my **Weddings** magazine features a variety of incredible cakes in every new issue.

Both cakes were attractive, but in the end it was clear that one sold much better than the other.

The lesson the **Apprentice** teams learned is that it's most important to see your Big Idea through the eyes of your customers. If you have a dream of starting a wedding-cake business, your survival and success will be built on selling wedding cakes to as many couples as possible.

Seven necessities for assessing your business idea

Developing and refining ideas for a successful business is exciting, and that is a very Good Thing. However, there is much serious work to do. Think of yourself as a scientist in a lab coat, and slide your ideas under a powerful microscope. It is time for examination. You must realize that ideas for new products or businesses have to meet a specific set of straightforward but important criteria.

1.

IS YOUR IDEA BETTER THAN ALTERNATIVES ON THE MARKET?

When deciding whether or not an idea is strong enough, important enough, and viable enough to become the foundation of a good business, you must determine if that idea offers advantages to customers. In other words, is the product better than the customers' alternatives? Does it have the ring of originality? Here is a case in point. Because I do a lot of entertaining, I have many sets of glasses, but I still keep my eyes open for one that may have a unique shape or design. I recently found such a glass, made by a company in Seattle called glassybaby. These small, round tumblers have modern lines, a heavy base that conveys good quality, and they come in wonderfully bright and cheerful colors. They are also versatile: fun for drinks, but equally lovely as votive candle holders or small flower containers. These glasses brighten up my more casual gatherings, and their distinctive look and feel made this a very good idea for an entrepreneurial business. Another glass company might find success by creating a glass that is resistant to spotting or breakage or perhaps by developing a less costly method to produce extremely high-quality glasses, making them perfect for mass-market distribution. These kinds of ideas could also lead to success.

2.
IS YOUR IDEA SIMPLE FOR YOU TO DEVELOP AND SIMPLE FOR CUSTOMERS TO UNDERSTAND?

Simple ideas are the most compelling and the easiest to sell, and I think that my first book, **Entertaining,** is a good example of this. It has a one-word title that tells the reader exactly what the book is about. If you want to learn about entertaining and doing it well, then you know that this book might be useful. Once you open the book, a focused yet lavish display of hundreds of ideas, recipes, and pictures will likely convince you.

When you are starting out, it is wise to keep your ideas focused and manageable. You do not want to become overextended. It is far better to start out slowly on a firm foundation with one great idea and build from there.

The process of simplifying an idea or several ideas is similar to editing written text. Gather your thoughts, and write down every possible element involved in developing your idea: design, color, packaging, manufacturing, employee training, sales and distribution, and so on. Ask for input from experts and friends. Next, begin the editing process, crossing out elements that complicate the picture or overtax your resources. Then determine how to deliver the most value to your customers with the resources you have. You will need a simple, clear message about the value you are offering to them, so resist clouding the message with too many promises and too much information.

If you develop a business called the 24-Hour Locksmith, your customers will know exactly what it is you do. It is clear from the name that they can expect 24-hour service from you. However, if you are growing an interior design firm that also imports exotic orchids and Persian rugs, it will be much more difficult to effectively market your business. Be patient and limit your offerings at the start. First create that essential Big Idea, then build on it one step at a time.

3.
ARE YOU IN A GEOGRAPHIC LOCATION WHERE YOUR IDEA WILL WORK?

Most people could surmise with very little effort that opening a swimming pool company in Anchorage, Alaska, is not a very good idea. However, many people do not appreciate the more subtle contributions geography can offer to the success of a business. Sara Foster, a very gifted chef, worked for me in my catering business years ago. It was clear then that this woman was entrepreneurial and on her way to something personally satisfying and monetarily successful. Sara is now the respected author of several cookbooks and the owner of two gourmet markets in North Carolina. One thing that really impressed me about Sara's early foray into business was how meticulously she researched potential locations.

She found and hired a demographer who gathered comparative information for her, such as population, income levels, growth potential, and other important elements, to equip Sara with the tools she needed to pick the right neighborhoods in the right cities. This information was well worth the investment. Sara's wonderful Foster's Markets are in Durham and Chapel Hill, North Carolina. That places them near Duke University and the University of North Carolina, where they attract a nice mix of food-loving people. Sara happily tells me, "I can look out and see mothers with strollers, doctors coming in between shifts, and students with laptops."

There are many other geographic considerations to be aware of when starting a new business. Are the suppliers for your materials nearby? If you are opening a mail-order business, are there affordable warehouse rentals for your merchandise? What are the shipping considerations? Keep in mind that parking and traffic patterns are critical factors to a retail operation's success. A business located on a one-way street, for example, may pose a real problem to customers trying to find you. Manhattan is a huge market for paint, but interestingly, Sherwin-Williams executives have explained to me why they do not have many stores in the city. Paint cans are heavy and unwieldy to carry, so unless you can provide parking right next to your establishment, it is sheer folly to open a paint store.

Finally, you must consider factors such as weather and humidity. You should be aware of seasonal visitor patterns. For example, if you plan to open a boat-rental business at a summer resort, will your business survive when the summer visitors leave? Or if you dream of becoming a custom home painter, what sort of guarantee on your work could you offer in humid Atlanta or, for that matter, in hot, arid Arizona?

4.

IS YOUR IDEA AFFORDABLE?

Many successful businesses start out small with very little capital. In Silicon Valley, there is a long tradition of "garage" inventors, such as the late Bill Hewlett and David Packard. These men started out puttering around in their garages, putting inexpensive parts together with soldering irons. The company they ultimately created, Hewlett-Packard, is now legendary in the world of computers. Similarly, breakthrough software products have been invented by people of vision working at home alone in front of their personal computers. And if you happen to know a most determined woman cooking away in her kitchen, do not underestimate what she may be stirring up.

There are other business ventures, however, that demand significant investment before the first customers appear. Retail stores require leased space, utility payments, alarm services, liability insurance, and, of course, inventory and sales personnel. And certain service businesses, such as dry cleaners, call for expensive equipment. You must be realistic about your resources and make a careful study.

I'll mention, again, my first entrepreneurial venture. There is an enormous difference between opening a catering business and opening a restaurant. I made a profit on my early catering jobs even though I was charging just $12 to $15 per person because I was operating out of my own kitchen. For each affair, I rented the necessary tables, chairs, linens, and place settings and figured those expenses into what I was charging. I knew exactly how many people I would be serving, and I purchased food and drink accordingly. I impressed upon my kitchen staff to be very careful how they used ingredients, right down to how little to trim off the ends of green beans and how to slice the tomatoes with the smallest amount of waste. As I grew, of course, I had to invest in equipment and hire more employees, but I did not take on debt. I was able to grow my business by reinvesting my profits.

Be realistic and frugal; be practical and clever.

5.
IS YOUR IDEA TOO BIG?

I did not start an omnimedia company in my kitchen at Turkey Hill; I started a catering company. What I learned from that business and from my previous jobs became the foundation and launching pad for everything else that followed. I did not try to make it all happen at once. I spent 7 years as a caterer before I felt confident enough to branch out. And when I did, I tapped that expertise to write books and magazine articles until I was ready to launch my own magazines and television shows.

Many entrepreneurs take on too much too soon or address too large a market with their first ideas. Even experienced executives with capital to spend often make the mistake of targeting too large a market, without proper messaging or without the ability to execute the highest-quality products. An interesting example is the grocery delivery company Webvan. Webvan had a good, sound idea but did not survive its "too big, too soon" expansion and its loss of focus and control.

Looking to expand very rapidly to head off competition, Webvan bought Home-Grocer.com, a rival company that was growing gradually while offering a very useful service to busy homemakers. I'll remind you of my horticulturist friend Dan Hinkley, who advises his students not to buy expensive trucks and backhoes until they secure the capital to afford them. Webvan bought vast numbers of trucks. They built large distribution centers to provide rapid response to orders from online customers. They needed hundreds of qualified drivers and deliverymen and encountered a labor shortage. As a local grocery delivery business, HomeGrocer had been a big enough idea. Webvan became **too** big an idea, practically overnight. Without enough customers to support its huge mountain of expenses, it failed. I wonder where all those cute little trucks are today.

6.
CAN YOU EXPAND AND EXTEND YOUR IDEA?

My definition of a Big Idea is one that may start small but has the potential to be expanded, to develop into something much larger. In other words, it has potential for leverage, which means that any investment you make only adds value beyond its original purpose.

The structure of Martha Stewart Living Omnimedia (MSLO) is probably the single Biggest Idea that ever came to me. We have a solid core of original and valuable information (we call it content) about living that we develop constantly, updating and enhancing and expanding all the time. In addition, we have a number of various media platforms, allowing us to package and present this information in ways that our customers find useful. For example, I can use a recipe developed for our **Everyday Food** magazine (current circulation 850,000) and prepare it on my television show, reaching a broader audience (10 million viewers). That same recipe may also end up in a book that we publish, so that it is now available to anyone who missed it in the magazine or on television (average book sales: 500,000 copies). That same recipe can be discussed and promoted on our Sirius radio channel, and it can be distributed over the Internet on marthastewart.com. And the fact that we are acknowledged food experts because of these great and useful and practical recipes means that people seek out our kitchen products, which are available at retail stores.

You would be impressed to see how, at MSLO, expertise in very specific areas leads to ideas that offer our customers knowledge throughout our entire spectrum of media concerns. We once created a diagram (see page 67) listing all of our media platforms and traced how the little pansy flower had been covered in each one: Our magazine featured cupcakes decorated with sugared pansies; on television, I demonstrated how to apply pressed pansies onto paper, creating lovely stationery; on my daily radio show, I explained to listeners that the word **pansy** stands for thought and remembrance; the syndicated newspaper column described how to press and dry pansies; customers could purchase a kit for making pretty glass pansy coasters from the Martha by Mail catalog; and at Kmart, one could find pansy seeds and live pansy plants for the garden.

You do not have to be a large company to

leverage your ideas. I have explained that it is not good business to launch your idea when it is too complex or has too many diverse parts. Going back to my example of the interior design firm, if you start out small and build your good reputation as an interior designer, once you are established and making money, you may leverage that fine reputation and begin offering your clients those Persian rugs that you dream about manufacturing or the line of decorative sconces your customers want and need so badly. After all, importing, designing, or licensing rugs under your name could very well be a complementary business once you have a solid customer base. The key to building a new business is to amass a core of repeat customers who trust what you offer in your primary business. These are the people who will be pleased to consider any fresh ideas you may present. They are also the people who will spread the good word when they are happy with what you provide.

ONE IDEA, MANY PLATFORMS

to teach ·································▶

MAGAZINE	BOOKS	NEWSPAPER
Long-form stories on single subject, with photography	In-depth treatment of single core area with photography	Short-form Q&A on single basic subjects with photography
⋮	⋮	⋮
▾	▾	▾
Pansy cakes	**Arranging flowers with pansies**	**How to press pansies**

·································▶ *to do*

RADIO	TELEVISION	PRODUCT	INTERNET
Single idea audio tips with transcript (90 sec.)	Single idea video segments (3–10 mins.)	Live Pansies Pansy Coaster Kit	Plant encyclopedia Archival
⋮	⋮	⋮	⋮
▾	▾	▾	▾
Spring bouquet for a friend	**Demonstration on how to press pansies**	**Involvement Martha Stewart Everyday Martha Stewart Signature Martha by Mail Martha's Flowers**	**Interaction Breadth and immediacy of information and products for individual action**

7 .
DOES YOUR IDEA MAKE THE WORLD BETTER?

A truly great Big Idea has all of the attributes I have already described, but it also has something else that makes it unique. It has that special "something" that affects people in a most positive way. At MSLO, we get feedback from our public when something we have done has touched their lives or changed the way they feel about something. It may be menu ideas for creating the perfect holiday dinner or decorating ideas for creating a very charming baby nursery.

J. K. Rowling certainly made the world better with her Harry Potter series. She is a fabulous and gifted writer possessing a most fertile imagination, and she is most definitely a brilliant entrepreneur. Look at what she did: In an era of television, video games, and Internet distractions, she single-handedly enticed millions of children to read—children who might otherwise have never discovered what a fabulous world awaited them inside a book.

A great idea is sometimes pulled out of the air

I wish I could tell you exactly how to go about finding your Big Idea, but from the examples I have shared, you can see that Big Ideas blossom in many different ways. One thing I have learned is that it is important to be really spontaneous: When you see or think about something that sparks a creative thought, capture it! I often use e-mail as a log for ideas; it is wonderful because it is so immediate. I also carry a paper notebook when I travel so I can sketch designs or jot down ideas; I tear pages from magazines of rooms or furniture or gardens I like; and I take photographs when I see something that appeals to me, its form, its color, or its potential function. I now have more than 1,000 folders that catalog my ideas—and assistants who help me organize them. If you keep an open mind and are receptive to suggestions from others, Big Ideas are everywhere. They are swirling all around us. Here is an example of someone who literally plucked her Big Idea right out of the air.

VICTORIA KNIGHT-MCDOWELL
Helping herself, helping others

Victoria Knight-McDowell was passionate about her teaching job in Carmel, California. She loved her second-grade students, except for one thing—they kept sharing their colds with her. In the early 1990s, Victoria decided that it would be a good idea to begin supplementing her body with vitamins and herbs in hopes of staying healthy. She spoke to fellow teachers and to air travelers who also complained of frequent colds. They, too, were taking various supplements, but Victoria began to wonder about the best combination to keep colds at bay.

By day, she taught her rambunctious 7-year-olds. By night, Victoria dove into studies on cold prevention, reading as much literature as she could find on homeopathic options. Then she went into her kitchen and became something of a chemist, mixing cocktails of vitamins, minerals, and herbal extracts. She eventually hit upon a winning recipe, which, to her delight, kept her cold-free for 2 years!

Encouraged by her own success at staying healthy, Victoria was able to see the big picture: Not only could teachers and airplane travelers benefit from such a product, but so could office workers, commuters, health club members, shoppers, and just about anyone who spent time in crowded locations. Of course, it is common knowledge that frequent hand-washing can prevent many colds, but hand-washing is not always practical. Victoria knew there was a gap to fill. She and her husband decided to market her Big Idea. Her formula took the shape of a pleasant-tasting effervescent tablet, which they named Airborne—a simple, easy-to-remember name conveying both the threat of the problem and its origin. As an herbal remedy not claiming to cure colds, the supplement did not require Food and Drug Administration approval or evidence of formal testing. This made developing Airborne practical and affordable.

The first preparation of Airborne was sold to a local drugstore in 1997. Less than a year later, Trader Joe's, a grocery store chain, ordered 300 cases. The business took off, and to Victoria's delight, Airborne is now sold at Wal-Mart, Rite Aid, Jewel-Osco, and drugstore.com, as well. Today, the business has sales in the tens of millions of dollars.

When I was first introduced to Airborne, it was quite clear to me that the idea behind it was compelling. Although her products now reach a very large market, Victoria started her business small and only gradually added new products to the line. As an entrepreneur, Victoria Knight-McDowell can feel proud that she helps not only her fellow teachers, but also scores of other people to avoid the annoying common cold. Not bad for an idea pulled from the air.

Get a telescope, a wide-angle lens, and a microscope

Martha's Rule 3

CREATE A BUSINESS PLAN THAT ALLOWS YOU TO STAY TRUE TO YOUR BIG IDEA BUT HELPS YOU FOCUS ON THE DETAILS. THEN REMAIN FLEXIBLE ENOUGH TO ZOOM IN OR OUT ON THE VITAL ASPECTS OF YOUR ENTERPRISE AS YOUR BUSINESS GROWS.

MANY FLEDGLING ENTREPRENEURS manage to get specific elements of their new business figured out very nicely but neglect other aspects that can jeopardize the entire effort. A successful entrepreneur cannot become so entranced with a grand vision that quality is neglected or so consumed with details that the competition is ignored and strategic or marketing blunders are made.

As you plan the launch of your business venture, close your eyes and imagine that there are three sorts of optical instruments on your desk and that, in the course of launching and running your business, you will constantly be switching among them. First, you need a telescope—think of it as a reminder to always keep in mind where you are going, your future. You need a long-term plan for how you are going to get from where you are to where you want to be. You need to separate the future into manageable sections and plan each in detail. Next, you need a wide-angle lens so that you can evaluate the broad landscape in which your business will operate—your competition, larger social and economic trends, issues related to suppliers and manufacturing that you must contend with but that you cannot always control. Finally, you need a microscope, because from time to time you must bore down to the finest details and force yourself to deeply understand the mechanics and nuances of your business. All three of these views—telescopic, wide-angle, and microscopic—are essential to business success.

By nature, I am a very curious person. My fans know that I love adventure. It gives me great pleasure to tour the aromatic kitchen of a bustling bakery, questioning each baker about what he is creating; to stroll through a lovely English garden, asking the gardener about specific species or cultivars; to work alongside a Chinese cook fashioning all sorts of dim sum with nimble fingers; or to discuss the trade secrets of woodworking with a fine craftsman. At the same time, I sincerely enjoy donning a hard hat and maneuvering along catwalks to tour a warehouse or a manufacturing facility; I find it deeply gratifying to trek through the enormous printing plants that turn out my books and magazines.

I also love seeing how our suppliers and partners, or potential partners, do things. I once toured the cavernous distribution facility of Amazon.com with Amazon CEO Jeff Bezos. Walls and walls of books, cleverly organized, spread out before us, and I could not help but marvel at the speed at which the order retrieval, packing, and shipping operations worked in concert. (Jeff, a brilliant marketer, has refined the concept of online purchasing so that it is now a most convenient way to shop without ever having to leave home and comfort.) I am just as fascinated to visit the factories where my Signature line of furniture is manufactured, engaging in shoptalk with the talented people who turn our designs into beautiful tables, chairs, and sofas. Not only do I relish the excitement of these adventures, but it is also very important to me to understand as much as I can about how things are made and how things work, especially when I discover a system or method that sets a standard for excellence.

You, too, must come to love all the key elements of your new business so that you can build a solid, well-designed operation. And at no time is it more important to understand the little details that make the Big Idea viable than when you are developing your vision statement and your business plan.

Your vision statement should be a clear, concise description of exactly what you intend to offer to your customers, emphasizing the special qualities you can bring to this business. For example, it might be something as simple as this: "SuperHot Sauces creates and sells spicy, full-flavored barbecue sauces for the restaurant trade. Created in our kitchens in Santa Fe using fine habanero peppers and other traditional southwestern seasonings, SuperHot Sauces will be available to restaurants throughout the United States, distributed through premium restaurant supply companies." Or you may need a vision statement for a service business: "Career Acceleration is a personal career coaching firm that offers midlevel executives the tools to better package, present, and market their skills. Through workshops, one-on-one coaching sessions, and practice presentations and interviews, Career Acceleration can help both private clients and executives referred by large organizations fine-tune their personal presentation styles."

Notice that these are brief, informative descriptions that convey the what, how, and why of your business but also speak to its aspirations, target market, and quality. They whet a listener's appetite to learn more. It is important to describe your business consistently and confidently when talking to all sorts of people. In the venture capital world, they call these sorts of descriptions "elevator pitches," meaning that if you happen to find yourself riding in an elevator with someone who might be interested in investing, you need to convey all the important details in less than the minute or two that you will have his or her attention! Depending on your type of business, it may also pay to develop a richly illustrated brochure early on that includes your company's aspirational mission but also speaks to the quality and content of your products. This type of brochure can be especially effective to take to customer meetings and to provide to all of your employees so they thoroughly understand where your company is going and what it stands for. That's exactly what we've done with our vision statement for MSLO.

Contained within a beautifully printed

brochure, our vision for our company and our commitment to our customers follows.

Martha Stewart Living Omnimedia is the leading integrated content company devoted to enriching the changing lives of today's women and their families. Our community of how-to experts is committed to teaching, innovating, designing, and inspiring with ideas and products that make every day more meaningful, more functional, and more beautiful. We elevate the familiar elements of daily life, infusing them with the pleasure and confidence that come from the growing sense of mastery and discovery we foster in our customers and ourselves. Our products and our style are distinctive, with a consistently high level of quality. Though our content is timeless, we deliver it in the most current ways: wherever, whenever, and however our customers need and want it.

**Martha Stewart Living Omnimedia:
Sharing the Good Things, every day.**

"Assemble your materials":
Make a business plan

So many of the instructions in my magazines and books begin with the simple phrase "Assemble your materials." I became acutely aware of this commonsense approach when I started cooking from Julia Child's **Mastering the Art of French Cooking.** I realized that if I did not read the recipe thoroughly and assemble all of my ingredients first, then the result very well could be a disaster. French chefs actually have a phrase for this, **mise en place** (MEEZ ahn plahs), which means "to put in place." In other words, have all your ingredients prepared and ready to go before you start cooking. You never want to begin a recipe only to realize halfway through that you don't have one of the key components.

In business, you don't follow a recipe; instead you need to formulate a well-researched business plan. Such a plan will help you assemble the information and strategies necessary to organize and build your company. There are many resources out there to get you started, some of which can be accessed right from your home computer: Score.org (www.score.org) is a national network of retired and working business professionals who volunteer their advice to small businesses in all stages of development; they also have offices where you can meet an advisor one-on-one or attend a workshop. Another online resource is the US Small Business Administration (www.sba.gov), which offers general information on starting, financing, and managing a business; the SBA's Women's Business Center (www.onlinewbc.gov) has information on grants and also contact numbers and addresses of Women's Business Centers around the country.

After you've done some initial research, share the first draft of your plan with people who can help you refine it: family, friends, mentors, other businesspeople, as well as accounting and legal professionals.

Don't hesitate to ask for help

I confess I never wrote a business plan when I started my catering company. Knowing what I know today, however, I certainly would never advise anyone to naively forge ahead without one. Writing a good business plan forces you to think realistically about what you are stepping into and will clarify what kind of help you need to find. For example, if you are confused with financing issues, you could speak to someone at your local Chamber of Commerce about where to find a reliable accountant, or you can ask the commercial loan officer at your bank what factors they take into account before extending credit. If your business involves turning a homemade item into a manufactured product, thoroughly research your manufacturing options and perhaps hire a manufacturing agent.

Here is an example of a sound business plan that really took off and one I am especially happy to share with you.

JOELLE HOVERSON
A strong network of support

Behind a turquoise-colored storefront on Sullivan Street in Manhattan's Soho district is a small shop named Purl. You may have guessed from the spelling that it is a knitting shop. During its hours of operation, the store is filled with customers and knowledgeable employees sitting around a communal worktable while knitting, laughing, and helping each other with their works in progress. Surrounding them in this cozy retail space are floor-to-ceiling cubbyholes that hold colorful yarns with extraordinary textures. Customers flock to the store throughout every season to purchase the wonderful fibers, patterns, and notions that are so artfully displayed.

The proprietor of this lovely boutique is Joelle Hoverson, a painter at heart who earned a master's degree in fine arts from Yale University. Joelle worked at my magazine as a stylist and was known for her keen eye for color, design, and style. A number of years ago, **Martha Stewart Living** published a story that inspired Joelle to learn how to knit. As a stylist, Joelle found herself traveling around the country with the magazine's camera crew. On photo shoots, in her free time, she would pick up her needles. When she could break away, she also visited the local yarn shops. It did not take long for Joelle to realize that she had her Big Idea. With all the myriad shops she had visited, she had never come across the perfect knitting store. There was always something that was not quite right: the selection of high-quality, natural fiber yarns was too limited; there was not enough teaching available; there was little or no feeling of community in the shops; and so on. It finally dawned on Joelle that she should open the kind of store in which she would like to shop.

On the advice of friends in the business world, Joelle researched the knitting market as a first step toward formulating her business plan. The Internet proved to be a good place to start. Joelle found dozens of Web sites devoted to the interests and needs of a vast community of knitters. As she suspected, knitting seemed to be enjoying a remarkable resurgence. It was also online that Joelle found contact information for suppliers of yarns and knitting supplies, whom she called on for facts and figures relevant to the business. She discovered that yarn sales were booming and that patterns and books on knitting were almost impossible to keep in stock. She realized that many others shared her new passion. The emotional connection to this old-fashioned pastime was catching on, and it was vividly clear to Joelle that it was time to consider the "market opportunity" section of her plan.

Throughout her years of employment, Joelle had managed to save some money to invest. However, she knew she needed to raise more to accomplish her dream. She prepared herself by creating a clear diagram of her potential expenses and sought advice from mentors and friends already operating small businesses. She walked through neighborhoods where knitting shops were nonexistent, looking for suitable locations, and she studied the pulse of those areas. She updated her plan, showing it not only to dear friends from whom she could expect unflinching support, but also to experienced businesspeople who would scrutinize her forecasts and point out where she had been overly optimistic.

Eventually, Joelle found what she felt was the perfect location. She wisely took the advice of a New York shopkeeper friend who urged her to sign at least a 10-year lease on the space in case the real estate market suddenly became hot.

Joelle properly planned her business launch. She repeatedly discussed the pros and cons of her venture with many people. In the end, her fortitude won out. Joelle quantified the success of her business in the following way: Purl is now open 7 days a week, and Joelle employs at least eight people, several of them full time. She has worked with vendors to create new colors for some of their yarns. She expanded the business by partnering with her sister Jennifer. Together they created their online store, www.purl-soho.com, which has more than 10,000 registered users—and counting. Joelle has even written a gorgeous book called **Last-Minute Knitted Gifts,** which is now in its fourth printing. By carefully knitting together a business plan, stitch by stitch, with help from friends and trusted advisors, Joelle has emerged as an entrepreneur with a successful first venture.

Here is the important point to remember: You can become so easily fixated on the attractive or most enjoyable elements of your plan that you overlook some of the more mundane but important details that will make your business work. Asking people for help will give you valuable perspective. And remember: **mise en place.** Have all of your ingredients in place, ready to go, before you start. And never lose sight of the big picture, the scope, the structure, and the details of your business.

Take time to save money

I have already told you about the brightly colored tumblers that I love, made by glassy-baby in Seattle. Lee Rhodes is the founder of the company, and she, like many entrepreneurs, was so excited about the enthusiastic response to her products that she did not sit down and sketch out a proper business plan or consult with professionals who could have helped her with key decision-making. She was feeling very good about the business she was building and thought that speaking to a financial planner might somehow take the soul out of it.

Lee personally took on a high-interest loan for her company instead of seeking start-up capital from a bank or looking for investors. That error created a higher than desirable debt burden. Lee ruefully admits, "I didn't have any business experience, and I was very cavalier about the financing." It took longer than anticipated, but Lee's business is now strong, and she has a beautiful shop where she sells her lovely tumblers.

The way to invest wisely in your business is to consult with a good accountant and a good lawyer to discuss what it is you wish to accomplish. Outside recommendations about procedural and developmental decisions can really aid a budding entrepreneur.

Rebecca Congleton Boenigk, who is now a talented and successful entrepreneur, learned that lesson the hard way. Rebecca is head of Neutral Posture, Inc., a Texas-based office chair company. This 16-year-old business started in the family garage. Rebecca's father developed special chairs that reduced pressure on key areas of the body. The designs were based on research gleaned from the US space program, which found that the body naturally assumes certain positions when in a gravity-free environment. Rebecca and her mother thought that these extremely comfortable designs would make perfect office chairs, and they started to market them as such. The company grew and grew, achieving great success. At one point Neutral Posture was even traded publicly, making it the only woman-owned and -operated company listed on NASDAQ at that time. For various reasons, the family decided to buy it back and took it private again.

Neutral Posture is a complex manufacturing business, and Rebecca had to learn a really important lesson before she built it into the successful enterprise it is today. In her words, "There are three must-haves: a great lawyer, a great accountant, and an insurance policy. We made horrible mistakes early on by not having stellar people in these three areas because we thought we could not afford it. We lost more money making bad decisions than it would have cost us to get the best advice upfront."

Whether you are starting out or building on your business venture, Rebecca's counsel is worth remembering. Losing money at the start because of false economies or bad or mediocre professional advisors could very well discourage you from forging ahead.

Rebecca has another piece of advice that I

find powerful: Never make a big decision without sleeping on it, whether it is a hiring decision or a strategic decision. "A lot of entrepreneurs think a day is too long to wait. But then you wake up a day or two later and go, "Oh, no," and spend just as much time undoing it. I can be an emotional decision-maker, but I have never regretted taking a little time."

Stories like Rebecca's are probably far more common than Joelle Hoverson's well-researched launch of her knitting shop, although even Joelle sees where she could have done certain things differently. (Her father had warned that her budget would never cover the cost of the renovations she planned, and he was right.) Despite early mistakes, Joelle, Rebecca, and Lee were determined to make their businesses succeed, and they did—proving that incomplete business plans or setbacks may slow you, but they certainly do not doom an enterprise.

Expand your range of vision

Seriously underestimating your startup costs is a common mistake among entrepreneurs. They may focus on big-picture costs, such as building rentals or vehicle prices, only to neglect lesser expenses such as utility bills, staff salaries, or local business taxes. And they almost always underestimate what kind of marketing investment is necessary to build awareness and create a demand for the product.

When Sara Foster, my wise and gifted former catering chef, prepared to open her first Foster's Market in Durham, North Carolina, she took great pains to write a thorough business plan. If you recall, Sara was also prudent in hiring a demographer to analyze the market for her. Within her plan, she figured out detailed expenses, right down to her projected monthly phone bill. She shopped around for the best insurance rates and factored those in, as well. What startled her, however, was discovering that zoning and local regulations regarding food handling and serving can vary dramatically from place to place, even between cities and towns within the same state. For someone who would rather be baking an authentic New York crumb cake or putting up a batch of savory seven-pepper jelly, zoning laws are very tedious details to consider.

Sara, however, was wise enough to research the regulations so that she would not have unwelcome and expensive surprises down the road. After all, what she really wanted to do was to create the best food possible to please her customers for many years to come. She did so and continues to do so.

Sara's diligent homework reminds me of another important item: addressing risk. Many entrepreneurs are so focused on their business idea that they fail to consider potential risks that could come between them and their dreams, much less think through how they will cope with those risks, should they arise. You must not become obsessed with what could go wrong. But you cannot be afraid to analyze the risks and threats you face from competitors, economic factors, natural disasters or the elements, or even from the inevitable mistakes and missteps that every business person makes. If you are beginning a luxury goods business, a downturn in the economy is a serious risk to you. If you intend to cater to tourists with a boat or bicycle rental business, one summer of unusually cold or rainy weather could be devastating to you.

Consider the risks

Perhaps you are a talented decorative house painter who specializes in marbling, faux bois, and other artistic finishes and are ready to launch your own business. You have every asset I appreciate in a good entrepreneur—you are an expert, you have enthusiasm, you have identified a service that many people want, you are operating in a high-net-worth area with access to a superb client base. What could go wrong? Well, do you have a good liability insurance policy? Paint is a wonderful thing when it ends up in the proper place, in the proper color, and appropriately applied. However, the fact is that paint can spill, bubble, crack, and even run at inappropriate times. Paint can be improperly ordered or mixed and not resemble what the customer wanted, requiring an expensive repainting. And, sad but true, painters sometimes fall off ladders or damage something in the home in which they are working.

Here is a disturbing but relevant story that was brought to my attention recently about an antiques collector who hired a firm to paint the interior of his home. Over the phone, he instructed the contractor to paint one wall in his kitchen—"the wall with the eagle on it" is how he described it, and, indeed, there was a massive bronze eagle with a 6-foot wingspan mounted on that wall. Imagine his horror when he returned home to discover that the painters had misunderstood the foreman's directions, and the gorgeous patina on his rare and valuable eagle was covered in a flat beige paint. If you are the painting contractor and this occurs in your third or fourth year of business, perhaps you can absorb the loss and carry on. Should you take such a blow on your first job and find that your insurance policy does not cover the restoration or replacement of such a valuable object, you may very well find yourself without any business at all.

Rebecca Congleton Boenigk has a similarly cautionary tale about the importance of insurance. A faulty electrical switch in her warehouse set off a very brief, very quickly contained fire early in her company's life. The sprinklers in a small, 10-foot by 10-foot section went off, and she thought damage was limited. In fact, smoke damage ruined her entire stock of fabric and foam for the chairs, and the water damage was far more extensive than it first had appeared, requiring floors and walls to be ripped out and replaced. Had she not had a good insurance policy, the damage, which came to $600,000, would have put her out of business.

Create a frugal culture

Let us assume you have organized yourself well and have gathered all the resources and followed all the steps required to launch your new business. Your trustworthy accountant and attorney have reviewed your plans and contracts. You have secured the requisite permits and insurance policies. You are filled with excitement and are ready to go. As you start to realize success, it is imperative to keep the following advice, which combines the big-picture vision of the wide-angle lens with the detail focus of the microscope.

No matter how extensive your resources, there must always be a budget, and someone has to be appointed to manage within that budget. If you are the founder, it is up to you to be the primary budget-minder. I am notorious for asking the people I employ about the cost of this or the cost of that: the price of a gallon of paint, the daily rental for a stump-grinding machine, or the expenses to cater a company luncheon. I expect very precise answers. This frugality is deeply embedded in the culture of my company. It is how I have always run my businesses and, in large part, why they have been profitable. It is not about being cheap but about being frugal.

Anyone who knows me knows that waste of any kind really bothers me. When I visit my office buildings and find air-conditioning cooling a large, unoccupied space, I adjust the thermostat. And why illuminate rooms that are not being used? Waste should bother you, too, whether you are launching a business or sustaining one. Make your employees acutely aware, from day one, that you intend to monitor spending. Encourage careful living and frugality both at work and at home where they live. Remember how I instructed my kitchen staff exactly how little to trim off the green beans? Waste often equals loss of profit.

Michael Dell, the founder of Dell, Inc., felt just this way when he started out. From the beginning, Michael knew that if he were to compete with already successful personal computer companies such as IBM, it would be crucial to keep costs as low as possible. But as the company grew and his managers were promoted to larger offices, he began to notice the furniture they were purchasing for their offices. Michael watched as it took several people to move large and expensive wooden credenzas through the hallways. He had never been fond of this type of credenza. He knew that decorative objects and personal photographs were placed on top of these office staples, but what exactly were the insides used for? When he inspected them, he discovered that most of the cabinets were empty. Michael made a company-wide announcement that there would be no more credenzas at Dell and ordered them removed from the building and resold to a used furniture dealer. In their place, he installed less expensive, more modern and functional pieces that reflected the nature and culture of his growing company.

This incident became known inside the business as the Credenza Wars, illustrating an important point: When you are trying to build your company, be concerned with the face you are showing to your customers. Michael Dell's Big Idea was to provide his customers with high-quality computers at the lowest possible price. He knew that conserving resources supported his Big Idea. I often say, "Make the world beautiful," and as a businessperson, I am speaking about the

customer's world. If you are running a decorating or design-based business, it is important that your space convey the taste and
sensibilities that you bring to your work so
that your offices, themselves, create a marketing vehicle. Similarly, if you are selling
personal computers directly to customers, as
Dell does, it is far more important that you
have low prices and excellent service rather
than a fleet of expensive, useless credenzas.
Once the initial idea, the business, is established, there is plenty of time to decorate the
offices. It's much easier to build a workplace
that is conducive to doing great business
than to build a great business. Concentrate
on the business first.

Be willing to adjust your focus

When I speak of the necessity of developing
a zoom in/zoom out focus ability, I am
not talking about micromanaging every
minute detail of the business yourself. What
Michael Dell did with those credenzas was
set an example. At that early stage of his

company's life, he was willing and able to pay attention to what was perhaps a seemingly minor issue in order to broadcast the very important message that waste matters. I am sure that he no longer has the time to concern himself with office furniture. He has, however, created a culture—a staff of similarly minded people—that can now do that sort of work for him.

MSLO operates in much the same way. As the founder of my company, I simply cannot oversee every tiny aspect of our operations. My employees, however, know my thinking and know what I expect. I have made sure that my executives understand how to manage and know and understand how to get things done. I set out to create a brand as well as a company, and that brand, I honestly feel, can be found in all aspects of my business.

Successful entrepreneurs have a keen focus and must remain true to their overall vision. They have the ability to change their focus from the big picture to the broad view. Their days are spent examining, thinking, rethinking. Recently, I spent my morning at the office reviewing long-term strategic plans with the executive team. Over lunch at my desk, I looked at the marketing and promotional plans for several upcoming product launches. That was followed by a meeting with the producers of my upcoming television show. Then I was off to the test kitchen to review recipes with the kitchen staff for a new food issue. After that, I was asked to look at colors and choose more than 400 new ones for the Martha Stewart paint collection at Sherwin-Williams—and you know how much I love picking paint colors!

I love my business—all aspects of my business. Whether it is picking paint colors or reviewing financial accounts, I find all these elements compelling. For a business to succeed, everything must blend together like the colors on those paint charts.

Teach so you can learn

Martha's Rule 4

BY SHARING YOUR KNOWLEDGE ABOUT
YOUR PRODUCT OR SERVICE WITH YOUR
CUSTOMERS, YOU CREATE A DEEP
CONNECTION THAT WILL HELP YOU
LEARN HOW BEST TO BUILD AND MANAGE
YOUR BUSINESS.

LET'S SAY YOU HAVE THE DESIRE for a good-quality prime rib of beef. You may decide to visit your local butcher, who selects a roast for you, weighs it, wraps it, prices it, and wishes you a good day. He is professional and courteous, and he sells a good product. But the two of you did not particularly connect. You might return to his shop the next time you are arranging a meal around a good cut of meat . . . or you might not.

Shop for meat at Lobel's on Madison Avenue in New York City, however, and you will have a very different experience. When you walk through the doors, you have the sense that you are walking back through time. There is simply no other butcher shop in New York like Lobel's. The shop itself is richly paneled in wood. Taxidermy deer and moose heads adorn the walls. The butcher area shines brightly with white enamel, spotless stainless steel, and sparkling glass. The cases are filled with plump, free-range, organic chickens; Long Island ducklings; quail; pheasant; milk-white, all-natural veal; exquisite lamb; Kurobuta pork; and the most succulent aged American Wagyu beef you could ever hope to eat.

Lobel's has been a family-owned business for more than 160 years. Its butchers, most of them bona fide Lobels, are unmatched in their knowledge about meat, a knowledge that they love to share with their customers. Evan is a nationally recognized expert on carving and has appeared on my television show several times, sharing his expertise. Stanley has coauthored six cookbooks and holds several patents related to butcher equipment. David left a lucrative career as a litigation attorney and returned to the family shop, where he tied his apron strings and joined the family and the business he loves.

Should you express interest in a Lobel's roast, you will discover that whoever waits on you will most likely ask you about the plans you have for dinner. They will inquire as to your preferences for taste and texture and the particular recipes you are considering. The Lobel's butcher will show you an array of meats that are solely USDA prime, for which less than 2 percent of the meats in this country qualify. When you make your choice, the store also will offer a selection of sauces, marinades, and even cookbooks that can help you prepare your meal. When they bid you a warm farewell, they also inform you of their Web site (www.lobels.com) in case any more questions arise when you get home.

Visiting Lobel's is a wonderful and gratifying experience, and you'll have the same sort of feeling if you visit them online. Their Web site is filled with so much helpful information, and the photographs of steaks, roasts, chops, and roasted chickens are so vivid that you'll imagine you can hear them cooking. There are numerous enticing recipes for all the cuts of meat that Lobel's sells and an extensive gift shop, where you can buy all five of their cookbooks, including **Meat,** which sold more than one million copies. Again, like **Entertaining,** the title is simple but describes exactly what the book is about.

Lobel's is a prime example of a business that embodies the single most important principle that I believe has fueled the success of all my own ventures, from my catering business to my media empire: Connect with your customer. The butchers at Lobel's love, cherish, and listen to their customers. They teach their customers everything they know so that they can learn from their customers how to serve them better. They can be satisfied that they are offering quality products that their customers truly need and, above all, want.

There are no people more important to me in my business life than my customers. My television programs connect with 30 million viewers per week. My magazines connect with 14 million readers per month. It is my responsibility to remind my employees that serving these valued and essential customers in the best way we possibly can is our number-one priority and the key to our success.

Extend the connections

When I was a caterer, I used every occasion to speak with my clients and ask them about the quality of their experience with me and how my service compared with other caterers. I wanted to hear what went right with the event that I catered and also what went wrong. From the comments my customers gave me, I was able to refine my products and services, to develop ways to further distinguish myself from competitors, and to gain ideas about how I might expand my business in the future.

Even as my business grows larger and more complex, the power of customer connections is proven again and again. We are constantly testing ideas with our customers and potential customers: We conduct polls over the Internet at least once per week on a variety of topics. We might e-mail five different images of a cover for one of our magazines, asking customers to choose their favorite. Or we might ask them to provide us with homekeeping problems that we could solve with our signature, how-to advice. The most wonderful thing about our Internet polls is that we receive as many as 1,000 responses in less than 30 minutes! And because our polls are so frequent, we can maintain strong, ongoing customer relationships.

Of course, we use many of the time-tested and more formal ways to solicit customer ideas and advice: focus groups that have helped us refine designs for our furniture, for example, and pilot-testing our new magazines, including the concept, names, logo, and cover design. When we are sure we have a product that is responsive to what our customers have told us they want and need, we will actually have a soft launch, where we sell the product in a select number of retail stores to see how it performs. We did this with **Everyday Food** before we launched it nationally.

I know many entrepreneurs who talk about their customers in a most caring and loving way. I have met others, however, who do not understand what it means to forge a deep connection. To be a really successful entrepreneur, you must constantly strive to understand your customers. You also must appreciate them and care about their happiness.

Ask yourself the following questions: Do you care? Does caring about your customer come naturally to you? If making money is more important than your customers' satisfaction and loyalty, then you may have not yet found the right business to build.

Love and concern returned

I have found, on a profoundly personal level, too, that when you truly care about your customers and pay attention to them, they will most truly care about you and your business. This was evident to me during my recent experiences with the justice system. All through the grueling months of my trial and later, during my stay at the Alderson Federal Prison Camp, I received hundreds of thousands of touching letters and e-mails full of support, encouragement, and goodwill. These messages warmed my heart. Just knowing that the many customers of my magazines, books, products, and television shows cared about me and had faith in me gave me strength and fortitude. These customers were not overly influenced by the negative press coverage I had received. I can't even begin to express how uplifting all that fabulous support was for me and the hundreds of people who work at Martha Stewart Living.

The last 3 years have been filled with so many unwanted distractions, but I have persevered, kept my optimistic outlook, and tried my best to keep in touch with all of my wonderful supporters. I started a Web site called **Martha Talks,** where I could communicate directly with my fans. I posted factual information regarding each day's trial proceedings, and I also let everyone know that, despite what I was going through, I was still thinking of them and their kindness. I was not about to ignore these loyal and caring friends. I have kept all those lines of communication open, and we are now inviting everyone who corresponded with me to sign up as guests on my new, live television show, **Martha.** We have been sending invitations out via the Internet, and our shows have been selling out within 2 hours.

When I was released from Alderson, I wore a beautiful, hand-knit poncho that one of the other women had made for me. That poncho was a symbol of the generosity and goodwill I experienced during my stay there. So I themed one of the upcoming segments on my new television show "Poncho Day"; we've received 10,000 requests for 164 places in the audience. Can't you just see how it will look in the fall in New York City—a line of 164 people wearing variously colored ponchos standing outside our studios on 26th Street?

Letters continue to pour in from supporters who tell me that they cannot wait to watch my new show. One such letter came from Jacquie McCully, who wrote: "I never had any doubt that you'd come back even stronger and better than before. . . . While you were away, I spent my months designing, building, and decorating my very own craft room; so I'm ready, Martha. I'll be tuning in." Maybe Jacquie will visit New York and come sit in our live audience. I would love it.

This kind of support confirms my belief that if you care about your customers, your customers will in return care about you and your business. Every successful entrepreneur I have mentioned in this book is fully aware of this fact. You can hear it in their voices; you can see it in their marketing and promotional materials. And you can experience it, for example, on Lobel's Web site, which is lovingly designed to inspire—and satisfy—pangs of hunger and an intense craving for steak at any time of the day or night.

Develop the appropriate attitude

Some people, such as good nurses and able teachers, are born with an ability to empathize. For others it takes a bit of time to develop the appropriate attitude. The advantage of starting a business in an arena about which you are passionate is that when you really care about something, as I do about cooking, gardening, and decorating, you can often serve customers very well by simply thinking about what you need and want yourself. In some cases, however, passion can develop from unforeseen circumstances.

RONN LANGFORD
On a mission to save lives

Consider the experience of real estate developer and former racecar driver Ronn

Langford. As a six-time Sports Car Club of America champion, Ronn focused his energy and passion on the mechanics of fast cars and on developing the proper skills to drive those cars for maximum performance. His racing "customers" were his sponsors and his fans who wanted to see his car driven to a winning finish. After Ronn's daughter was killed by an intoxicated teen driver, however, he cut back on his racing and founded the MasterDrive Teen Driver Survival Program, based in Denver, Colorado, which teaches crash avoidance and defensive driving. Ronn's school has grown and expanded to focus on other high-risk groups, and he now also teaches senior citizens how to be more alert and able drivers.

Because of his terrible loss, Ronn felt he was on a mission to save the lives of other teens by teaching them how to properly handle themselves in cars. To him, it was a matter of life and death. Unfortunately, sometimes his concern and strong belief in the value of what he was doing actually prevented him from connecting with his customers. "I guess I would call it a misguided passion," Ronn explains. "I would go into schools and circulate flyers about our teen driving program, and parents would call me and the first words out of their mouths would be, 'How much do you charge?' I would be furious that that was what they were concerned about. If your child needed a heart surgeon, would you call and ask how much the surgeon charged?"

Given the horrible ordeal that his family had experienced, his reaction was understandable. Many people would be unable to function at all after such a personal disaster, much less take their pain, frustration, and anger and channel it into something that promised to achieve so much good. Great credit to Ronn for establishing a useful and needed school, but even he began to realize that his anger was getting in the way of effectively marketing this important service.

His attitude was also preventing him from reaching the teenagers he was so eager to turn into good drivers.

Fortunately, Ronn altered his thinking and refocused on what he was trying to do. He shed his defensiveness and did a 180-degree turn in the way he approached his potential customers. "There are 6,000 teens who die every year in traffic accidents, and there are 300,000 who are seriously injured," Ronn explains. "But I finally realized that even parents don't understand the dynamics of putting a 4,000-pound car in motion and how to properly control it in a crisis. I had to educate both parents and children." Ronn developed a free program called Beyond Blind Faith that explained the risks and the tragic statistics about teen experiences behind the wheel. Parents began to view his service as essential instead of expensive.

Last year, Ronn Langford's Master-Drive program trained 5,000 teenagers in life-saving techniques and brought in $5 million in revenue. There is now a related newsletter and a Web site offering information about safe driving techniques. People who have suffered brain injuries seek him out to enhance their driving skills. Because he was willing to let go of his personal anger, Ronn is now successfully educating his many customers and, in doing so, learning the best ways to expand what is now a thriving business.

Profit by giving information away

When I can arrange it, fly-fishing is a pastime that I really enjoy. My older brother, Eric, introduced me to this sport when I was a child. He loved puttering around his favorite tackle shops, studying various lures, flies, rods, and reels. He was quite adept at tying his own authentic-looking flies. He loved the camaraderie he felt with other fishermen. And, of course, he loved to tell his fish stories, which I think are half the fun of this sport. Any good tackle shop owner understands this very well.

Perhaps you are a passionate fly-fisherman and your Big Idea is to open a tackle shop in the heart of bass- or trout-fishing country. You have determined that there are many people in your area who share your enthusiasm for fly-fishing but must drive great distances to purchase fishing gear. You also know that your location is a vacation spot, and there is a demand for guided fishing trips. This seems like a recipe for success.

So you open your doors for business. Fishermen stream in, and you are faced with a dilemma. Your customers want to talk to you about fishing. Some of them will buy gear. Others have come only to look. You still have boxes to unpack, inventory to organize, vendors to call, and ads to write for the local publications. You realize that friendly chitchat about water temperature and barbless hooks is consuming precious time. Plus, if you give away all your knowledge of the best local fishing spots, how will your guide business make any money? How you interact with these potential customers can make or break your business.

The smart fishing entrepreneur loves the sport himself and understands that his shop is going to attract people like my brother, Eric. To connect with his customers, the owner could post a daily chart that reports on local stream and lake fishing conditions and identifies those flies that seem to be catching fish. He should also have a Web site that consolidates this information and maybe offers regular advice on using different flies and other tackle. He may offer an electronic newsletter that he encourages every customer who visits his shop to sign up for. The smart shop owner will make every customer feel important. Even if he cannot take the time for conversation, he will refer every customer to his other resources so that these patrons realize he is sincerely trying to help them have a good fishing experience. When customers know you care about them, you will acquire allies who will help promote your business. When you are willing to share useful information, you might find that local publications are calling for your reports about fishing conditions. If they print your expertise and mention the name of your business, you are getting free publicity.

The successful fishing entrepreneur understands that, though it may seem counterintuitive to give away valuable information to potential customers, he is not undermining but rather broadening his business. Not everyone can afford a guide or wants a guide, but the smart shop owner knows that by providing useful information, he is building his reputation as an expert and an important local resource. The higher the regard in which his customers hold him, the greater the chance that when they wish to hire a guide or simply buy bait or tackle, they will think of him first. That is how the smart business owner builds a customer base.

We offer the same kind of service through our Web site, where we have archived 3,600 free recipes that can be searched by categories such as healthy living, children's meals, and holiday menus. These include three delicious recipes devised by my daughter, Alexis: for sweet potato pie, chopped vegetable salad, and her famous brown-sugar chocolate-chip cookies, which millions of people have baked and loved. We provide other information to our customers, too, such as our favorite tips on gardening, cooking, and homekeeping.

This is such good business sense, but so many businesspeople neglect this important piece of the equation. They fear using precious energy on things for which they do not perceive they will be compensated. I am not saying to spend lavishly, by any means. I am saying, however, that you must be willing to make that investment by connecting with your customers. On their Web site, Lobel's generously shares some great recipes. They also sell their cookbooks. If you do not understand the customer connection, you may wonder why customers buy Lobel's cookbooks at all when they can get some of their recipes for free. The smart entrepreneur, who understands what customer connection is all about, knows that by sharing with the customers, more products will sell. Bond with your customers; forge that connection!

Paint a happy picture in which your customer appears

Here is another scenario that may take place at the tackle shop. You open your doors early on a Saturday, and a gentleman enters who wishes to browse. He observes your daily fishing report and engages you for 15 minutes of animated talk about fishing conditions. Finally, he gives a sigh and tells you that he promised his wife that he would spend the weekend doing yardwork. After he leaves, all he can think of while pushing the lawn mower is your enthusiasm, telling him of the 2-pound bass people were catching at the lake. When he finishes mowing, he asks his wife if she wants to go fishing. Your door opens again, and there he is, back in your store, buying tackle and other gear, getting a map, and hiring a guide for him and his wife for the very next day.

Great entrepreneurs are both smart and optimistic. They are willing and able to paint a picture for their customers, depicting how much better their lives will be if their customers subscribe to the entrepreneur's ideas or buy their product. Great entrepreneurs should and do truly believe in the transforming quality of what they are selling or offering.

On my television show, when I am creating a recipe or demonstrating a craft, I do so in a way that I hope conveys enthusiasm and pride for the finished product. After all, I sincerely want my viewers to try these things, and I sincerely want them to succeed. I believe they know this about me. Customers are not dumb; they can sense when you are insincere. This heartfelt sincerity is what will separate you from your competition. As in the Domino's Pizza example, you do not have to be the first or only fly-fishing shop or guide service, but you must prove yourself to be the superior alternative to any other tackle shop or guide service. You must be the expert, displaying your passion for fishing, and you must care deeply about your customers' experience.

Customers are your best consultants

Have you ever felt ignored or neglected by someone with whom you have done business or are trying to do business? Perhaps you have had these feelings in a restaurant as you stand by the hostess station trying to get seated and are pointedly ignored for no apparent reason or at the customer service window of a department store, where you are told it is your fault that some product malfunctioned. I will share one such incident with you.

I am driven to the city every day by a driver. I choose, for a variety of reasons, to sit in the front seat. I use drive time to talk on the telephone, e-mail on my Blackberry, read the daily papers and correspondence, and even to apply my makeup, for which I need to look in the mirror. But when I drop down the visor and lift the mirror cover, I am very annoyed that this mirror is not centered properly for the passenger. Instead of reflecting my image, I get a good view of the backseat. I must lean over or sit in the center of the front seat to see myself, which is difficult to do while wearing a seat belt, not to mention inconvenient. I realize that the designer of the visor and mirror may not apply makeup, but he or she has violated the first rule of product design: Imagine and know how your customer will use the product.

What to do? I personally have written letters to the car manufacturer complaining about the design, and I assume that others have done so as well. To this date, no one has written back to me, nor have they changed the design in their most recent models. Because I really like most of the other features of the vehicle, I have installed another mirror over the existing one so I can use it. This is just an example of frustrating a valued customer with bad design or just utter ignorance that translates to "not connecting, not caring" about the customer.

Connecting with customers is a mindset. If you make it a priority, it will become easier and more natural for you to do. Recently I found myself in two very productive meetings with design teams from Armstrong Floor Products and General Electric. With the Armstrong team, we discussed ways to make flooring even more appealing to their customers. The General Electric team was curious to learn what additional kinds of features new appliances should have to make life easier and invited me to visit their laboratory to discuss how to design them. One thing I know for sure: I don't want a talking refrigerator! I can see for myself when I am down to my last carton of milk. The people on these two teams asked very good questions, and I found them to be curious and forward-thinking. These are well-established and mighty companies who, not surprisingly, constantly think about new markets, new designs, new opportunities, and how to serve their customers better. And that is a large part of why they are so great.

When you are really interested in connecting with customers, complaints do not frighten or irritate you. Unlike the maker of my car, you should be happy to respond to your customers, listen to their complaints, and consider their suggestions. At MSLO, we answer every letter and every e-mail.

This is no small task, as we receive upwards of 500,000 letters per year. We now have a Letters Department to handle all the mail, but I still take home an assortment of letters every month from customers who are satisfied and those who are not. We feel that our customers are our most trusted consultants. They share their ideas and let us know when we veer off track. We pay close attention when we receive letters of complaint. It may be someone having difficulty with a recipe or someone who cannot find a particular craft material to complete one of our projects. We tune in to these letters because they teach us how we can perform better.

And sometimes we receive very poignant mail. David and Susan Segal wrote, "Just before Christmas last year, our house was destroyed by fire. During the chaos of picking up the pieces of our lives, my wife and I came across a copy of **Martha Stewart Living.** It brought order and a level of calmness to the peaks and valleys of depression that followed during the reorganization of our lives." When you receive a letter such as that one, it is deeply moving. You understand that you have reached a level of great meaning and importance to your customers. It serves as a reminder that it never pays to take the easy road or the less expensive, more expedient path. It inspires you to work at your job even harder.

Think like a customer

My mind is always at work, searching and thinking of ways to improve my customers' experience. That is how I was inspired to create our magazine called **Everyday Food.** In our flagship magazine, **Martha Stewart Living,** soon to celebrate its 15th anniversary, we have always provided wonderful recipes. We also display the food in the setting in which it will be eaten—at a formal holiday table, a beachside picnic, or an intimate setting for two at home. This is all part of that inspirational picture we are painting for our customers on every page of this informational magazine. It is about lifestyle—not only what to prepare, but also what to serve it on, what to eat it with, and where to eat it. The magazine presents recipes and food in a visually exciting and emotional context.

But because we diligently read all of those hundreds of thousands of letters from our customers, we know that we also connect with another important cooking audience through a very popular feature in the magazine called "What to Have for Dinner." There are many busy, active readers who love to create delicious, nutritious, complex dishes but don't have much time. Along came my Big Idea for **Everyday Food.**

I was actually harboring this idea for quite some time. Years before, while visiting friends in London, I happened upon a very nicely printed, beautiful magazine at Selfridges, an upscale store in London. The magazine sold for just a pound (at the time about $1.20) and featured ingredients available on the shelves of the store. "Brilliant idea," I thought. The size was approximately the size of **Martha Stewart Living,** and I thought that if it could be made smaller, pocket size, it would be even more appealing and useful to me and others. I remember thinking that if we could find the right advertisers, we could work with them so that the advertisements not only would support the publication, but would also educate readers about their products. We could and would provide recipes using the thousands of ingredients readily available in American supermarkets, encouraging healthy, good, nutritious, simple, quick everyday cooking in everyone's homes.

I knew that such a magazine would be appealing to our loyal readers, but I had a strong suspicion that it would also attract an entirely new set of patrons: families with children, young professionals, students, and men who want a healthy and satisfying meal that is easy to shop for and easy to prepare. I also knew that this magazine could make the world better. I think the public is realizing that processed foods and fast-foods, convenient as they are, are not necessarily healthy or good for us and our children.

I brainstormed with my staff, and in the late 1990s, we began developing our new magazine. We really worked hard on this project with the strong belief that **Everyday**

Food would be less about dreaming and more about doing. This new product was to be useful, practical, and functional. **Martha Stewart Living** is so successful because we have created a formula that works for us. We realized that now we would have to invent an entirely new formula. We put together a small team of editors, cooks, recipe developers, a chief art director, and a few food stylists. The rules for this team included creating new, delicious, and simple recipes that could be prepared in less than an hour and that used no more than 10 easy-to-find ingredients per recipe. The small, compact, digest-size format of **Everyday Food** allows it to easily slip into a pocket, handbag, or backpack, making it convenient to carry around a grocery store.

When we sketched possible design themes, we already knew from their letters that this new customer base preferred a photograph of the finished dish on the same page as the recipe. Scot Schy, the new art director chosen from the staff of **Martha Stewart Living,** developed an efficient, clean layout that we call "the recipe spread." It lists ingredients, displays the recipe, and places a strong, beautiful, illustrative photograph close by. There are also numerous photographs of many recipes in their preparation stages. I explained to the team that I wanted this magazine to embrace the very specific journey from the oven or stovetop to the table. I wanted the food to look as it would for our customers in their homes.

Let me stress one final point about connecting with customers and holding them in high regard. We never talk down to our readers of **Everyday Food.** We do not think of them as lesser cooks than those who purchase our other cooking and entertaining products. After all, we at MSLO have many busy employees who love to cook from **Everyday Food** on a regular basis. They are living the life we are writing about, and **Everyday Food** helps them do that. We keep in touch with our customers because we **are** our customers. We know that they, like us, want a little extra something; so in every issue, we include informative tidbits such as "Have You Tried . . . ," which introduces the readers to new, possibly exotic but useful ingredients such as sesame oil, feta cheese, and mango chutney, and we give suggestions for using them.

I am very proud that our little magazine has grown rapidly and has won lots of awards. Most important, our readers love it. We receive positive feedback daily. Ann Nann of Jefferson, Massachusetts, recently wrote, "Your magazine has made my grocery shopping easier, and I have been a lot more energized to make dinner." Loyal and happy readers inspire us to be as creative and energetic as we possibly can when thinking up and designing new products.

See beyond the initial transaction

To expand and build your business, you must extend the impact and influence you have in your customer's life beyond any one transaction. You need them to view you and your business as their primary resource, their refuge, their reliable provider of information, products, entertainment, or inspiration.

Here is another scenario. You decide it would be a good idea to open a laundry pickup and delivery service. While doing your business research and planning, you ask many people about their laundry habits, how much they pay, and how much they would be willing to pay for pickup and delivery convenience. To your surprise, you find out that nearly everyone dreams about such a luxury, but only single, working professionals are willing to pay your prices. So you launch a service that travels to office buildings on a firm schedule, exchanging clean and crisply pressed garments for soiled laundry on site. This commonsense approach enables you to access the customers most willing to pay for your service while limiting the time you spend driving around, making this venture more manageable and lucrative. Employers may even embrace the idea of permitting you to enter their premises, offering this service, because they may feel that by doing so, they will appear more sensitive to their employees' personal needs.

There is so much more to building and expanding a business than just adding more customers. You can instead offer your current customers more services. For instance, if you are successfully running a company that cleans carpets and rugs, you may want to add carpet repairing and upholstery cleaning and repairing services. Your customers know that they can count on getting value from you. They will keep listening to you for your advice on helping them improve their lives, and they will give you their ideas on how to be even more successful in making them satisfied customers. It is a win-win situation.

I have mentioned my admiration for what J. K. Rowling accomplished regarding the Harry Potter books. Although authors are not necessarily thought of as entrepreneurs, I feel that Ms. Rowling is a very smart one for a number of reasons. First, she understood her readers so well, and she created not just one, but a series of books that continued to deliver to her readers the elements they so enjoyed. This was not as common or as easy as she made it look. More frequently than not, authors find it difficult to follow up a first novel, particularly when they attempt to write something very different from their first success. Many times sequels disappoint. Ms. Rowling stuck with the elements of her stories that she understood her customers loved the most. She did not introduce new sets of core characters, nor did she send Harry on a long escapade through the nonmagical world. That does not mean that her subsequent books were not creative and fabulous, because indeed they were. And she did not simply churn them out. Rather, she took the careful time that she required to make each magical in its own way. She understood that her original Big Idea connected so profoundly with her customers that she continued to portray her characters' adventures in hair-raising conflicts and uncanny predicaments that she knew would appeal to her fans.

The Harry Potter series was the heart of her Big Idea, but she knew that idea could expand in a number of ways, most importantly into winning, box-office-hit movies. She made certain, with close observation, that the quality of those movies was in keeping with the rich, complex details of her books. She also created an enormous licensing business for related products that continued to grow with each new book.

We know that customers are happy to respond to entrepreneurs and businesspeople who demonstrate that they truly want their customers to have a good experience. This is true whether it is reading a book, mopping a floor, or accessing information via Google or Yahoo. This is such a simple, straightforward concept that it makes me wonder why so many businesspeople are neglectful of the customers' needs and wants.

All dressed up
and ready to grow

Martha's Rule

USE SMART, COST-EFFECTIVE PROMOTIONAL TECHNIQUES THAT WILL ARREST THE EYE, TUG AT THE HEART, AND CONVEY WHAT IS UNIQUE AND SPECIAL ABOUT YOUR BUSINESS OR SERVICE.

AFTER YOU'VE COMPLETED YOUR RESEARCH, formalized your business plan, and are finally ready to launch your new venture, or when you've determined that the time is ripe to introduce a new product or take the next step in building your established business, you will need to spread the word about your new product or service. To do this effectively, you need to consider all the methods of convincing the consumer that your product stands out, whether it's in packaging, advertising, publicity, or, ideally, all of these. I have found that the two most important elements in your promotional strategy should be creativity and common sense. A successful business absolutely needs both.

When it comes to promotion, creativity without a commonsense approach is usually an expensive failure. What good is an advertising campaign in which the actors, slogans, or punch lines are more memorable than the product being promoted? What good is the message if it is so obtuse that consumers cannot figure out what is being sold? On the other hand, common sense without creativity is simply boring. I have seen perfectly good business plans fail because creative directors could not figure out how to make the company shine brighter than competitors selling similar products or services. Marketing is expensive, time-consuming, and people intensive; and you do not want to waste money on costly mistakes.

On the other hand, with clever, unexpected advertising, you would be surprised how you can make something sell. Take a look at the approach used by Subway sandwiches. Subway developed an attention-getting campaign that featured a young man who had shed quite a few pounds eating a Subway sandwich every single day. The advertisement caught the attention of Americans who wanted to lose weight, and it was effective because the message was unexpected, even counterintuitive. Here is another classic example. Back in the 1970s, Colgate-Palmolive wanted to distinguish its dishwashing liquid from others on the market. They created Madge, the manicurist, to promote Palmolive as a product that not only cleaned dishes very well but also was gentle on your hands. These memorable television ads featured Madge's surprised clients discovering that their hands were actually soaking in Palmolive prior to their manicure. Campaigns like these are simple yet highly effective because they convey hidden features that distinguish a product from its market competitors.

The goal of your promotional efforts is to have your product or service stand out from others on the shelves in creative, interesting, and attractive ways. For example, I have a massive line of Martha Stewart–designed Everyday products that are sold at Kmart in the United States. Many of these products are familiar, basic items such as glassware, tableware, cookware, and kitchen gadgets. We have made sure that our product quality is excellent because we want the customers to know that every dish is high quality, every towel is manufactured to strict specifications, and every lamp is designed with great style. We have gone to great lengths to ensure that the packaging conveys that special quality and style. Our design team created sophisticated, upbeat packaging, using bright, modern colors and a pleasing typography. The labels and boxes mirror the packaging for more expensive products and reinforce the value that our brand represents: heirloom quality products—products that will look just as wonderful years from now as they do today. That is why you will find our packaging to be identifiable but

not trendy, stylish but practical and durable, and instructive. Every frying pan, for
example, comes with recipes as well as suggestions for product care and use. We
suspected, and found to be true, that our
Kmart customers are delighted that they can
purchase quality merchandise, so nicely
packaged and affordable. This marketing
strategy helps our customers to feel good
about their purchases and be proud of their
choices.

Package it right

When considering how to introduce your
product to the world, you need to think of
how to make it most presentable. You must
give it the proper name and the right image.
What will its logo be and how will you
package it? When deciding on a logo, do
not get stuck trying to invent one as iconic
as Steve Jobs's apple or Ralph Lauren's polo
player. Rather, look to capture your company's uniqueness: its own nature and scope,
its personality, its style. And remember that

your company will likely change and evolve, so consider a logo that ideally can evolve, too. The best name and logo for your business should reflect the sum of its parts—what your company is and stands for now and what it aspires to be.

Good packaging arrests the eye, attracts the heart, and perfectly suits the product being promoted. Lee Rhodes of glassybaby packages and promotes her hand-blown glass tumblers with the most wonderfully designed graphic cards, showing her glasses in all their many glorious colors. Her packaging, printed cards, and Web site are all simple, colorful, joyful, minimalist, and most effective. Lee has also given her colors very creative names. Envy is a rich shade of green; Tang, a vivid orange like the drink; and True Love, a palpitating red.

Victoria Knight-McDowell also employs colorful packaging to set her Airborne tablets apart from traditional, over-the-counter cold remedies. She and her husband embraced a fun, casual, cartoonlike theme; and they prominently feature the fact that the product was developed by a teacher. A further promotional touch is that the name **Airborne** doubles its appeal, suggesting both the germs it protects against and the travelers who need it most. Plus, customers find the slightly homemade look of the packaging to be quite endearing.

There are agencies for hire that specialize in image design, product and company naming, packaging, and other elements of promotion. At MSLO, we often work with such people to help us market and promote our various products, but we have also, as we have grown, created a marketing department all our own to design everything from logos to packaging to advertising to radio and television commercials. Your company may very well grow to a size where one day you will have such a department filled with professionals. At the beginning, however, using common sense and creativity, you can start modestly and lay the groundwork for a strong brand with promotional efforts that are neither grandiose nor extremely expensive but that can be quite effective all the same.

Position your product or service

While you are considering what kind of compelling image might be appropriate for your company or new product, you should take into account its positioning in the market. This is the perfect time to gaze through your wide-angle lens. Ponder what exactly you are trying to accomplish or trying to sell and how your product or service will be better than others already out there. Are you targeting a mass audience or an elite, upscale niche within that broader market? Is your product one that sells on an emotional or impulse basis, such as gifts, food treats, or beauty items? Or is it something that buyers will want to know certain specifics about, such as electronics or power tools?

For example, if your company's vision statement is "We intend to become the worldwide leader in customized, elegantly designed iPod cases, sold directly to consumers via catalogs and the Internet," then your promotional positioning should be something distinctive, such as "We are the only company that produces custom-designed, fine leather iPod cases for sophisticated, adult music lovers who appreciate classic styles." In this case, your product positioning defines what is different about your product (you are the only seller of custom leather cases); the value of your product (custom designed, high quality); and the nature of your customers (sophisticated, adult music lovers).

Doing this exercise can lead you to the appropriate name and logo, which, in turn, influences the style of packaging and promotional materials you need to develop. There are many companies out there making iPod accessories. Most of the cases offered are made of high-tech materials, addressing a youth market, and those are price competitive. Your product is clearly going after a different market segment, a more refined consumer, and that should be reflected in a more sophisticated name, logo, and marketing style. For example, your promotional materials will not feature a teenager in baggy jeans and a baseball cap, but rather a stylish man or woman riding on a commuter train and listening to an iPod enclosed in an elegantly tailored leather case. You are clearly positioning your iPod case as a luxury item, even a fashion accessory.

The Target brand presents an interesting case in creative repositioning. For years, Target was just another mass-market discount store, selling products that could be found in many other places. Then the marketing department had the brilliant idea to sell Target as the "in" place to shop, the "fun" store, the "cool" store, the "avant-garde" store. For several years, the promotions promised more, much more, than the Target stores delivered. But the campaign continued, and the company followed up by commissioning high-profile designers such as Todd Oldham to infuse their products with a certain style. It took awhile for the chain to deliver on the promise, but the marketing plan worked, the promotional gamble paid off, and today's Target customers are more than happy with the stores.

Appeal to your customers' wants and needs

Advertising is an extremely powerful and essential tool for successfully promoting most products. Because it is usually expensive, it is really important to analyze what sort of advertising will work best for you. You must decide which vehicle will best convey your message to the people you desire to reach. If you are selling tools or electronic equipment, for example, your ad should emphasize the utility and particular specifications of your product. If you are trying to lure customers into your new bakery, you may wish to purchase advertising space on the sides of buses, where a mouthwatering photograph of your baked goods can appeal to hungry pedestrians' impulses.

Again, both creativity and common sense are of utmost importance. Cyndi Stivers, an executive at MSLO, shared a wonderful story of how she and her team promoted a new magazine, **Time Out New York,** on a very limited advertising budget. While walking on Astor Place, the crossroads of the East Village, Cyndi's staff noticed that the Public Theater had a blank wall facing the bustling intersection, and an idea occurred to them. **Time Out** would offer to paint a large ad for the theater's new show on that wall, including a prominent reference to the magazine and its logo. A brilliant idea! For the cost of a few hundred dollars in materials, **Time Out** got its name in front of thousands of people every day because it convinced the Broadway show of the wisdom of sharing this brick "canvas" benefiting them both. In another smart, creative promotion, **Time Out** custom-printed their logo and marketing message onto paper coffee cups. The cups were distributed to coffee vendors throughout the city neighborhood where major advertising firms are located. For several weeks, the name, **Time Out,** was literally right in front of advertising buyers' noses at minimal cost to the magazine.

I think that most really great advertising represents at least one call to action: It will make you think, make you try, make you shop, or make you buy. Some of the best advertising campaigns include more than one of these principles. That was the case with our launch advertising for Martha Stewart Everyday products at Kmart. The ads played with the idea that this was no small endeavor; I was featured driving a Kmart 18-wheel delivery truck, drying luxurious sheets on top of the dramatic, red and gold boulders in Sedona, Arizona, and even draping the sheets to form a long, undulating fence like a Christo art project. The unexpected and often humorous situations certainly got the attention of television viewers—and the obvious quality and value of the featured products enticed people to shop and buy.

Beyond marketing:
the publicity game

I have always believed that advertising should go hand in hand with publicity, which some people think of as free advertising. In reality, it is not free because it demands your time, energy, and intelligent planning to be truly effective. Publicity is different from advertising because it entails capturing the media's interest in your business. Very often the best way to accomplish this is by being aggressively bold.

Local newspapers and television and radio stations are always working on special-interest stories that require local expert information. If what you do is respected and commented upon by customers, chances are good that reporters and producers will call on you for your expertise. You may not be able to promote your product or your Big Idea every time out, but you will be building relationships that will help you over time.

Let's go back to the example of the tackle-shop owner. His business would be well served if he had the confidence to send out a letter to all the local media outlets offering his services as an expert fishing source. "When you are working on any story related to fishing," his letter might read, "I will be glad to make sure you get the best and most current information."

Once he has made such a media connection, he should keep his eyes peeled for new developments that might be of interest to local fishermen and be ready to suggest them to reporters as story ideas. Perhaps a new lure has been introduced that is making the locals ecstatic. Or maybe an environmental issue is threatening local species. If he can write or talk knowledgeably on these topics, he can secure some valuable publicity for his store. He should also be willing to reach out to the public. For example, his tackle shop might host a Learn-to-Fish Day, teaching local children how to cast, or offer to put on a fishing clinic at local schools. Or he could raise money for a local environmental charity by organizing a fishing derby. By all means, he should inform the media of such events. Photos of children's events are a staple of newspaper feature sections. Every time your business is mentioned and you are quoted, you become more recognizable, and your company's profile as a local resource grows.

This same practice holds true for a service business. Perhaps you are a teacher who has personally built a well-respected private tutoring business. You wish to expand by opening a tutoring company that helps high-school students prepare for the SAT exams. Contact all the local reporters who deal with education stories. Talk to your local radio and television stations. Be generous with factual information about education, testing, or college preparation. Give them suggestions for story ideas that will attract the attention of parents, who are, after all, your potential customers. Develop a way of describing how your tutoring program is more effective than others, and even invite those reporters to observe you in action. These are the kinds of stories that the media needs to cover. If you view reporters and editors as your customers, as well, and think like they do, you will make a connection. Eventually, when your business is flourishing, you may wish to hire a public relations person to shape your story for maximum exposure. When you are starting out, though, you can build your own profile if you have the courage to put yourself forward.

When I was starting my catering business, I let all my friends who worked for the local papers in on the news. I encouraged coverage by hosting parties, donating foods to charity events, and even holding cooking lessons for the young school friends of my daughter. These classes had a twist—the children were not necessarily taught just simple basics, but more complex techniques and classic recipes. Each child could turn out a perfect omelette, make a tasty, paper-thin crepe, and concoct an excellent soufflé by the time they "graduated," at 10 years of age. The stories I generated were terrific, with lovely photos and lots of recipes. It was the kind of public relations practice that I continue today with a company listed on the New York Stock Exchange.

Promote yourself as an expert

Perhaps your Big Idea involves selling a handmade craft, and you are wondering what you can do to be considered an expert. You might ask yourself these questions.

1 .

IS THERE IS A COMMON PROBLEM PEOPLE FACE THAT YOUR BUSINESS HELPS SOLVE OR A SEASONAL ASPECT THAT YOU CAN USE FOR PROMOTIONAL PURPOSES?

Everyone loves it when his or her problems are solved and solved well. And few people dread a season of the year more than "tax time." If you have opened an accounting firm and are trying to promote its business, develop a creative way of talking about it, such as offering the local media the chance to discuss "the five most common mistakes people make during the year that will come back to haunt them at tax time" or the "five often-overlooked deductions that can save you thousands of dollars." You might even offer to prepare a reporter's tax return for his story to illustrate these points. Concentrate on basic, universal problems to help connect your solutions with other peoples' problems.

Stories tied to a holiday are another great way of generating news coverage. For example, by mid-November, newspapers are printing stories with suggestions for unusual and unique holiday gifts. If you feel that your handmade craft would be a desirable gift, a well-prepared press release with photographs is one way to get the reporters' attention. Another good way is to send the product itself with an explanatory letter and an excellent photo that the papers can reproduce. If you can have the photographs scanned and send the press release in an electronic format to make the information more accessible and editor friendly, all the better. Let them know why your product is special and why it makes a good gift. Keep in mind that holiday stories are written well in advance of the holiday, and the papers need lead time.

2.
WHAT ARE THE SOCIAL DYNAMICS THAT HAVE CREATED THE OPPORTUNITY FOR YOUR BUSINESS?

Maybe you are launching a therapeutic massage company, and you come across a medical report about how regular massages can help ease back pain. Send it to your local newspaper, pointing out that there are some excellent local massage therapists, namely you, who can help readers to explore this option. Invite them to send a reporter with a backache or a stiff neck (the entire staff will volunteer) for a demonstration massage. Pamper the press, and they will help you.

One of the reasons I wanted to create **Martha Stewart Living** magazine was because I perceived a social trend: It was perfectly clear to me that women were hungry for information to help them run their homes more efficiently, entertain with more ingenuity and style, and learn all the clever homemaking techniques and tips that their mothers may not have taught them. I made it a point to discuss and promote the notion that "living" encompassed much more than just decorating and cooking—that it also embraced crafts, collecting, gardening, cleaning, organizing, and inventive child rearing. Raising the notion of homemaking to an art rather than treating it as a chore, made me different and interesting and worth covering for the press. In the beginning, reporters treated me a bit skeptically, trying to understand the multitasking I talked about, the joy I experienced, and the enthusiasm I exuded when I discussed what I was working on. But the more I talked, the more books and magazines I sold, and I became known as an expert in homekeeping and all subjects related to living well. In the process, amazingly, homekeeping was elevated to the art form it deserved to be.

3.
CAN YOUR PRODUCT OR SERVICE BE EFFECTIVELY DEMONSTRATED ON TELEVISION?

Television has extraordinary reach and power, and with the ever-increasing number of cable channels, there are more—and more specialized—programming options available than ever before. There are channels that focus on animals, gardening, the home, food, and so many different topics, in addition to local, community-based shows that are always on the lookout for interesting people they can introduce to the hometown audience. Demonstrating your product on one of these shows can be a fun and valuable way to attract customers. Appearing on television is also an effective way to promote services, such as career coaching, particularly if you have an animated, friendly, jargon-free manner when illustrating your methods and their potential value to customers. Viewers love to see that you enjoy and believe in what you do. And they love success stories.

There are two reasons why I am so confident about this approach to promotion. First, it worked for me. As I became more and more well known through my catering business, my early books, my magazines, and later my products, I traveled widely, giving speeches on my areas of expertise. Sometimes I donated my time to a charitable organization to help them raise money, and sometimes I charged a speakers' fee. These events created a national audience for my subject matter, increased my customer base tremendously, and created demand for more Martha Stewart–related products. That in turn led to regular appearances on the **CBS**

Morning Show and NBC's **Today** Show. The exposure generated interest in my magazines and books and, later, my daily television show. I have mentioned the idea of "teach so you can learn." You must also remember the concept of "teach and the press will help promote you!"

The second reason for believing this approach works is that in our magazines, newspaper columns, radio shows, and daily television show, my producers and I are always scouting for individuals who are expert in some fascinating area that can be shared with my readers and viewers. My good friend Melissa Neufeld, a clever California entrepreneur who built a very nice business featuring gorgeous gift-wrapping papers, decorative stickers, and handcrafted holiday accessories, was a frequent and popular guest on my television show. Melissa is adept at creating very beautiful items in a simple and easy-to-demonstrate manner. She agrees with my approach to promotion— she does not hide her special techniques or hold back on what she has learned. She realizes that, while some viewers will be motivated to create what she is demonstrating, many more will be happy to visit the gift shops that feature her wares and simply buy them. It pleased me to give Melissa exposure because I appreciated her friendship and her amazing talents and because she also brought much joy and many great ideas to my audience.

Get personal

Another thing to keep in mind is your personal story and whether it has ingredients that reporters will find intriguing, novel, offbeat, or funny. Perhaps, like Ronn Langford, the story of how you decided to start your business has a compelling emotional element. In his case, the notion that a distraught father found a way to help other families gives his enterprise an integrity and gravitas. In the case of Airborne, the fact that it was invented by a teacher has great public relations value, and the company has played up this angle brilliantly. We are a culture with a great fondness for teachers (although why this does not equate to a culture that more universally respects and values their endeavors escapes me), and the idea of any product being endorsed or invented by a teacher gives it instant credibility with the public.

I believe that each phase of my career has been intriguing to people in part because of what preceded it. When I was a stockbroker, people were interested to learn that I used to be a model. When I became a caterer and author, local media found it compelling that I had been a stockbroker. My image developed as a person who was willing to take risks and try new things. There are so many people who dream about changing their lives; the media know the public loves to be informed about someone who has dared to go out and do it.

Consider the elements of your life that people will relate to. Did you recently have a life-changing experience, such as a divorce or a death in the family, that convinced you to no longer put your dreams on hold? Did you suddenly find yourself so preoccupied with an idea—such as when Joelle Hoverson became enchanted with knitting—that you could no longer see yourself being happy doing anything else? Or did you simply observe an unmet need in a marketplace and know that you could be the one to fill it?

One tried-and-true way to attract the media's attention is to focus on yourself as the "face" of the brand. This has worked beautifully for Ralph Lauren, Donna Karan, Sean "Diddy" Combs, and Oprah Winfrey, to name a few—as well as for me. Becoming the face of your own brand is a very effective way of connecting with your customers. A friendly, attractive face attached to a brand is a powerful selling tool. But it can also be problematic and is not always the perfect "eternal" image for a brand.

One downside is that it requires a lifetime commitment. And if something unforeseen happens such as a serious illness, death, or even a lengthy, debilitating lawsuit, it can have a disproportional effect on your business.

Tell your story well

To be a successful entrepreneur, you must always search for ways to convey to potential customers all the good things you are doing. Writing **Entertaining** made me an instant expert on the subject. Because I was perceived as an expert, I made sure I could also speak well about the subject matter in my book in ways that media outlets found useful to pass on to their audiences.

Before you start sharing your information with the press, polish yourself by practicing on family, friends, or employees. Do this in a talk show format where the "host" grills you with questions. Develop your own question-and-answer script, but encourage your interviewers to be spontaneous, as well. This will familiarize you with listening carefully to interviewers' questions so you can grow more confident with practice. Remember to look the interviewer in the eye, try to relax and smile, and keep your answers relatively short and to the point. Do not underestimate the importance of your first interview with a small, local newspaper. Facts, figures, statistics—all of these should be as accurate as possible because the first printed interview in a local newspaper will often lead to interviews in bigger newspapers and magazines and eventually to radio and television, so you want to ensure that everything you say, everything that is reported, is true and not misleading.

At first, you will likely be the sole voice of your brand. As you expand and take on more employees, however, keep in mind that building a strong brand and accomplishing your goals means that you must be diligent in keeping your message consistent. Your goal is for your customers to associate your enterprise with a few important and memorable characteristics that only change if you deliberately decide to change them. The more that you and your employees sing the same song, the easier it will be for your customers to remember the principal melody.

Be consistent in your message

Another key factor in promoting your business or service—or even a nonprofit organization, for that matter—is to develop slogans and sayings that reinforce your brand messages. I am well known for saying, "It's a Good Thing," and "Learn something new every day," and "If I can do it, you can do it." At MSLO, we see ourselves as a teaching company with a deep commitment to helping people learn how to perform basic but important activities well. These sayings, which I repeat regularly, are constant reminders to my employees, customers, and the press what we are all about.

Consistency of message is vital. Recently, an acquaintance described how she helped a nonprofit medical clinic in the Southwest prepare a much more effective message for fund-raising. The clinic has been in operation for more than 30 years and has many outstanding and highly qualified professionals associated with it. They are all greatly dedicated to the mission of the clinic; however, they discovered that they had not articulated the strengths and values of the clinic to the community very well. Consequently, although the number of people seeking medical treatment at the clinic had increased dramatically, its donations had not.

My acquaintance, a communications specialist, gathered key people from the clinic and reviewed the kinds of branding considerations I have already mentioned: Who were their primary customers? Which organizations competed with them for the same philanthropic dollars? How were they different from competing nonprofits? What really was the value they provided to their patients?

She made it clear to them that it was not enough to talk about the quality of medical care or the nurturing nature of the staff because any similar clinic could assert those same claims. After much discussion, the workshop group decided to focus on the clinic's independence, which gave it flexibility to innovate and adapt to the community's changing health-care needs. They would pay attention to the comprehensive nature of its services, from prenatal through eldercare, and to the partnerships it formed with its patients for long-term prevention as well as short-term access to critical care. These three ideas—independence, comprehensive services, and patient partnerships— could be easily remembered by anyone who spoke on behalf of the clinic. Better yet, they could be well supported with data and programs that made it clear why the clinic was and is a unique and treasured community institution. This exercise has paid off: The clinic has raised nearly half of a multi-million-dollar, 3-year goal.

Special events help brand you as special

There are occasions when the sheer size of a well-produced event can generate comprehensive media coverage. For example, when we launched our Martha Stewart Everyday line of Christmas decorations for Kmart, we decorated 200 Christmas trees in our building with our products. We hung thousands of glass balls in the unique and rich colors of our line, and we generated dozens of tantalizing stories with photographs of the trees to spread the word. This was a time-consuming promotion, but it was not difficult for my staff, nor was it particularly expensive for the business. It did serve to announce, with our trademark flair and style, that our decorations were beautiful and unique.

For a company such as mine, it is easy to produce a large-scale event. But even modest events can be quite effective when attempting to launch a new business or reinvigorate an established one. You could throw a launch party and invite the local press, as Joelle Hoverson did when she hosted an opening party in her small knitting shop. She used all her resources and invited every magazine and photographer she had access to. She served delicious food from a neighborhood restaurant and wisely offered only white wine, not red, to prevent stains in her new space. She handed out printed material and information about yarn crafts at the door. Her efforts resulted in very favorable coverage in a number of media outlets.

Dealing with the press is far less complicated than many people initially believe. The key is to be patient and view the long-term picture. Most reporters are good and fair thinkers, and after many years of dealing with them, I have found that most are happy and willing to work with friendly, enthusiastic, and helpful people who have a story to tell.

Build your profile as an expert

As I've said before, I have had the good fortune to personally know many highly creative people who have been motivated to start their own businesses. Many of these entrepreneurs have raised their profiles as experts by writing magazine columns or books. If you can find a way to do this in connection with running your business, I highly recommend it. After I wrote **Entertaining,** I produced one book per year for

11 years. Each of those books expanded my profile as an expert in the various core content areas of my field of interest. Each one brought a new wave of publicity, which allowed me to talk about new ventures at MSLO and our contributions to the lives of homemakers everywhere. Sara Foster has written several cookbooks, as have the Lobel brothers. Dan Hinkley has two fabulous books to his name, and Joelle Hoverson created a gorgeously photographed and illustrated book on knitted gifts. This is another example of synergy in action. As an established expert, the media comes to you, and that media attention serves to reinforce your primary business.

A word on Internet promotion

In an extraordinarily short period of time, the Internet has grown into an invaluable promotional resource for businesses of all sizes. You can design highly targeted advertising that runs on search engine sites or related Web sites; and, of course, you can be very creative with the look and content of your own Web site to engage, amuse, and attract customers to your products.

By having a Web site, the teaching component of your business becomes easier and more economical. You can offer extraordinarily in-depth information on that site, information that would be expensive and clumsy to provide to customers in any other way. At marthastewart.com, for example, we offer a search function for recipes. This is much more efficient and cost-effective for us than having to send a recipe through the mail. Thousands of recipes are shared monthly via the Web site, but we will still mail you a recipe if that is the best way for you to receive your request.

You can also create inexpensive, lighthearted promotions, such as the brief, hilarious Internet videos we compiled to promote my new live television show. They juxtapose some of the more formal activities for which I am known, such as preparing elegant food or making a beautiful wedding cake, with some of the funny and memorable bloopers that have been filmed over the last decade while taping my show—such as the time I was pulled to the ground by a cow at an Easter party, or at the Chihuly Glass Blowing Studio when an enormous piece I was blowing slipped and shattered into a million pieces. Portraying me in this light is a fun and unexpected way to promote the new, live show, where we fully anticipate unexpected events to occur. We will just have to maintain a good sense of humor about such bloopers and inadvertent mishaps!

Even if you are the most technophobic businessperson running a small and efficient business, you cannot possibly ignore what the Internet can do for you.

Quality is everyday

Martha's Rule

QUALITY SHOULD BE PLACED AT THE TOP OF YOUR LIST OF PRIORITIES, AND IT SHOULD REMAIN THERE. QUALITY IS SOMETHING YOU SHOULD STRIVE FOR IN EVERY DECISION, EVERY DAY.

PEOPLE SOMETIMES ASK ME HOW I DEVELoped my particular sense of style and taste. My response is always, "Through comparison." What do I mean? Consider this example: The title of Master Sommelier is the restaurant world's highest distinction for a wine expert. To be granted this prestigious title, a candidate must go through a very lengthy process. Becoming a sommelier is not simply a matter of developing a sensitive palate and memorizing a restaurant's wine list. The certification involves multiple levels of courses, rigorous examinations, and blind tastings, all designed to make certain that the sommelier has developed the exquisite ability to assess the quality, character, and suitability of a wine with just one sip. Each new release of wine from the thousands of vineyards all over the world has its own complexity and nuances. A wine may be richly described as having citrus or berry top notes; chocolate or tobacco undertones; or a bouquet evocative of grass, cinnamon, or even mango. The Master Sommelier—there are only 120 in the world—appreciates the chemistry of wine-making as much as the vocabulary associated with describing wines; the growing of vines as much as the crushing of grapes; and the fermentation process as well as the blending. The Master understands how factors far removed from a dining table, such as the effect of aging in French oak casks rather than American oak casks, can influence a wine's ultimate quality and its value. This ability—this art—was acquired through a careful, masterful comparison of all kinds of wines, from the most exquisite to the rather mundane.

Like a Master Sommelier, a successful entrepreneur brings to the daily running of his business a heightened ability to both identify quality and also to understand what goes into producing it. The smart businessperson is always comparing designs, materials, and methods in order to offer the best quality experience to his customers. Whether you are alone in your field or have direct competitors, your devotion to quality will make you shine and set you apart from your competition. Quality equals happy customers.

Awards versus rewards

We have won a long list of distinguished awards at MSLO, including the highest awards in our primary fields of endeavor: the National Magazine Award and the Emmy Award. We are very proud of these awards. With such recognition, we might be tempted to rest on our laurels, but we know that awards are merely symbols. We have positive feedback coming in daily from our customers because they are happy with our products. **That** is our reward and the most important form of recognition we could hope to receive.

Today's world is terribly cluttered with dispensable, inferior, and even useless products. This is unfortunate for our environment as it contributes to the depletion of the earth's resources. But it is also a shame, because the customers who purchased those products did not get the highest quality possible for the price they could afford. Your business goal should be to learn as much as possible about every factor that affects the quality of your products and services. At the same time, you must create a corporate culture that embraces and produces quality at every level with equal fervor.

Put quality on a pedestal

If you peruse the pages of **Martha Stewart Living,** you will observe what happens when a group of creative, insatiably curious people who are obsessed with quality explore a topic. It is always about comparison. It may be potatoes or rolling pins, monograms or pinecones, scented geraniums or vintage quilts. Whatever the topic, all of us begin our exploration by creating a portfolio of styles, species, models, and flavors, illuminated by insight into the functional, tasteful, and beautiful attributes of each example we highlight. In editorial meetings, the editors of **Martha Stewart Living** are leaving no story angle unexamined before arriving at their ultimate approach. They take a team approach to this sifting because they absolutely care about bringing readers the most interesting, most informative, most useful, and most beautiful stories that they possibly can. My colleagues and I are all about quality and our stories reflect that.

In 1995, after 5 years of running **Martha Stewart Living,** I decided to make an important leap. By listening to our customers, by focusing on their needs and wants, my staff and I realized that many of them were having difficulty assembling various tools and ingredients featured in our pages in conjunction with various crafts, projects, and recipes. We realized it was time to extend our brand into actually designing and selling products—as long as those products would mirror the unchanging values and design vision of our magazines' content. I wanted the products to elevate and honor the broad span of domestic arts we featured, including cooking, entertaining, gardening, homekeeping, and craft-making. Just like everything else we were known for, these products had to help our customers do Good Things. While not necessarily inexpensive, they had to represent good value.

This was a groundbreaking, even stunning notion in the media world. At that time, other magazines' merchandising efforts had been restricted to mostly books, videos, T-shirts, calendars, and other promotional materials (sometimes referred to as "swag") that simply carried the publications' logos. We were determined to use our magazine stories as an inspiration for our products. We knew our designers could utilize their knowledge of manufacturing and merchandising to create product lines that coordinated and solved problems while at the same time providing better materials and better colors to enhance our customers' homes every day. Gael Towey, our creative director, refers to this approach as our "three-dimensional editorial" approach. All of these products would be sold through a catalog and online: The business was called "Martha by Mail."

Our very first internal product was a cake-decorating kit that we assembled from components we used to decorate the gorgeous cakes pictured on the pages of our magazines. These items—pastry bags, icing tips, spatulas, combs, and colorings—were packed carefully in an aluminum box, with a booklet of illustrated instructions.

We launched the catalog business, an online version of the catalog as well as an online greeting card business, and an online fresh flower business. We did wonderful, innovative things, such as make modern versions of vintage jadeite glass. Later, we came up with a marvelous cathedral cake pan, which updated a classic design, enabling the modern cook to produce a beautiful, sculptural dessert that did not require frosting. An additional and very welcome feature was that the pan could be washed in the dishwasher.

Other products followed: a cookie-decorating kit; oversized copper cookie cutters; all kinds of beading kits, craft kits, even sewing boxes.

What we brought, collectively, to the product designs was not only style and taste, but also our expertise. After all, our magazine stories are as much created as they are reported and researched. We develop recipes, invent craft projects, decorate rooms, and design wedding cakes. We realize the difference between poor-quality spatulas and garden clippers and the best. Because we do all of these things, we live the life of our customers. We know what tools we want and need; and we find them, design them, and make them if necessary.

Quality for the masses

These early efforts were very successful and most satisfying. In our catalog, we not only designed and commissioned many fabulous products, but we also edited an extensive list of existing products into a few that met our quality standards and that deserved to be featured in our catalog—such as my favorite gardening clogs.

In 1987, I had joined forces with mass-retailing giant Kmart to assist them with design ideas for home products, all of which were top sellers. At that time, Kmart was almost four times larger than Wal-Mart and many times bigger than Target. Ten years later, in 1997, I could see the potential for a much expanded home products line that could bring high quality to a mass market, most particularly to Kmart shoppers.

I was excited about the huge impact we could have on the American home. Using Kmart as the stage, we displayed our first designs for new bedding and bath products, which we called Martha Stewart Everyday.

We developed our own line of paint called Martha Stewart Everyday Colors. We soon expanded into Everyday kitchen products, organizing products, and window treatments. Later we added cookware, tabletop products, outdoor furniture, gardening tools, plants, seeds, our popular holiday products, and finally a line of affordable, good-quality, ready-to-assemble furniture for the home.

From the onset, I have been puzzled by some people's reactions to my association with Kmart. When this news was first publicly revealed, several speaking engagements on my calendar were actually cancelled—a Junior League member told me they were concerned that I was going down-market! I also had many conversations at gatherings that went something like this: "You have always stood for the finest in quality, the finest in presentation," a questioner would begin, carefully, somewhat self-consciously. "So why would you choose to distribute your products through a company best known for low prices and discount merchandise?" I would respond, smiling, "Simple. Quality does not have to be only for the wealthy. Mass markets matter. Great sales volume can enable better quality at lower prices."

It seems odd today, when many mass marketers have enlisted the help of famous designers to improve their product quality and style, that it took so long for people to catch on to these ideas that were clear to me almost 20 years ago. When I first became involved with Kmart, an extraordinary number of people—at the time, close to 70 percent of the country's households—shopped at Kmart's nearly 2,200 stores. As a businessperson and a person who cares about quality, I found the possibility of having an impact on such a huge market irresistible. Because of the reach of my magazines, television, radio, and other media platforms, I was already a mass-marketer. I had millions of readers, viewers, listeners, and customers of many different income levels and backgrounds. And I cared about all of them deeply, as I do today.

During the planning stages of the Martha Stewart Everyday line for Kmart, I listened intently to what my customers wanted. My staff and I had spent years informing them about how to make their everyday lives more satisfying through our magazines and our television shows. We taught them how to work more efficiently so they would have more free time to spend pleasurably. We showed them how to bring more beauty into their lives. Yet the kinds of merchandise available at lower price points in mass-market stores, was disappointing, to say the least. Before our Everyday line was introduced, a stroll through the bath towel aisles at Kmart revealed a depressing array of dark colors—predominantly maroons, forest greens, and black. The bedding aisles were filled with scratchy 50/50 polyester and cotton blend sheets and coverlets. I wanted to bring beautifully designed 100 percent cotton sheets to the marketplace and to improve the feel and texture of the blended sheets. And I vowed to improve the color selection and patterns to more accurately reflect the lifestyle we at Martha Stewart Living talked about and desired ourselves.

I knew that if we put forth our best effort,

we could offer something far superior. Manufacturing, distributing, and physically selling the enormous variety of goods I envisioned was far beyond our means. However, with Kmart's huge volume and power to negotiate less expensive manufacturing options, we could focus on doing what we do best—imagining and designing the products we knew our customers would love. We also made sure that we controlled the packaging and advertising of these products so that they were properly positioned and promoted.

Today, in collaboration with Kmart, we market superior products that most people can afford. I am so proud that we bring elements that had formerly been associated with high-end merchandise, such as high-thread-count 100 percent cotton sheets; plush 100 percent cotton bath towels in gorgeous, bright, and cheerful shades; and fine three-ply stainless steel cookware. Our team has now designed products for eight different collections: Home, Garden, Kitchen, Keeping, Decorating, Baby, Holiday, and Colors. These collections include tools as basic as clothespins (with a charming clothespin bag) and ironing boards (broad, sturdy, and very well priced), and as unique as a Japanese santuko knife that can cut food into paper-thin slices. The Martha Stewart Everyday line at Kmart is a celebration of good taste, fine design, and very good prices and an endorsement of the value of quality. It brought excellent-quality goods to a gigantic market that had been sorely neglected for many years.

Every business has a standard of excellence

All talented entrepreneurs develop both expertise and a finely tuned sense of what quality means in their particular field. Before she cuts a single hair, Eva Scrivo, my hair and makeup stylist, carefully studies each client's face and bone structure. She asks about their life-style and what they envision for themselves. After evaluating and assessing, Eva begins cutting, not following a faddish trend but a style she perceives is perfectly suited to that person's image and desires. Add that expertise to Eva's insistence that her customers be treated the way guests would be in her own home, and you have all the makings of a quality experience.

Fritz Karch, our collecting editor, is another quality impresario. Fritz is a devotee of all things old, all things "period," and all objects intrinsically beautiful. But Fritz does not stop at that. He has made himself an expert on the history, manufacture, and usage of all those things. On any given weekend, you will find him visiting antique shows, flea markets, and tag sales. I recently had a question about a magnificent chandelier I had purchased and needed to move, so I went to Fritz. With minimal description on my part, Fritz was immediately familiar with the style of the piece and its value— amazingly close to what I paid! He told me a bit about its provenance (he had seen it long ago in a shop in Maine) and advised me on how to move it safely and even how to best hang it in its new location. He has a keen eye for quality because he has a passion for endlessly comparing objects in a never-ending quest for the best. Fritz is the best of the best when it comes to collectibles in the world of antiques: the perfect student and the perfect teacher.

Putting it into practice

When creating a business, your concerns about quality should be included in your vision statement, such as, "We intend to create a chain of premier eldercare residential facilities, situated within the most modern and attractive surroundings, and offering the most innovative health-care services in the Midwest." Or it might be something much simpler: "We intend to bake and sell the finest macadamia nut–chocolate chip cookies in Honolulu." Statements such as these serve to remind you and your employees that the point of your business is to do something in a superior way. One of my favorite advertising slogans was the famous tagline of Federal Express: "When you absolutely, positively need to get it there, overnight." Given such a slogan and a deep commitment by management to make it a reality, it is no wonder that company's employees are famous for going above and beyond their duties to deliver their customers' packages.

There are many books dealing with the processes and management techniques that are supposed to produce quality. But books aside, I believe the critical point is for management to continually reinforce the quality message, making investments and decisions that remind employees that quality matters above all else.

Here is one important distinction for you to ponder when motivating your employees to respect quality and what it means. There are businesses in which quality is all about exactly following a precise plan. Perhaps you have opened a fresh juice company. Your customers order their beverages from a menu that includes very specific combinations and fresh, healthy ingredients. These kinds of establishments have stringent hygiene regulations involving the handling of ingredients and sanitizing of mixing containers.

Within your fresh juice shop, you are not looking for employee creativity. You do not want employees to substitute bananas because the peach bin is empty or to hand-wash blenders because the dishwasher is full and they want to go home earlier. Your management attitude must be unyielding. Insist on prescribed rules and techniques: "This is the way we do things. There will be no shortcuts taken. If you have ideas for a new process or product, present them to me. But if you like to take shortcuts and it threatens our quality, then you are working at the wrong company."

However, if you are operating a business that demands creativity and innovation, never discourage employees from experimenting with or presenting ideas before they are fully formed. A vague, seemingly mediocre idea can grow into a great idea—even a new Big Idea—once everyone starts thinking about ways to develop and improve it. You, as a manager, as a leader, must understand the need for trust and for brainstorming with your team. If you create the impression that an idea should never be mentioned to you, unless it is of peerless quality, you will shut down creativity as surely as if you had shut off the spigot on a faucet.

I am known for having high standards, but I also love collaboration and experimentation. I rarely enter any project with a rigid notion of what will ultimately produce the best possible results. I try to encourage people to express and share their ideas and opinions, to offer feedback, and then to critique the final project so we can attempt to do things even better the next time. You must nurture the minds and the confidence of your creative force. Without your support, they will be crippled, and where will that leave you and your business?

In Chapter 2, I discussed how widely and often we critique ideas as a way to refine those being developed and to encourage employees to offer future creative ideas. I believe so strongly in this concept that I often arise at four in the morning to send off a memo about the ideas discussed the previous day—what is promising or even brilliant and what needs further work—while the discussion is still fresh. If people feel comfortable playing with new ideas, they will come up with better and better concepts. But if you don't respond to your employees quickly, the ideas and your company's creativity will soon become stale.

When excellence takes a vacation

Have you had the experience where a trusted product, one you depend on, suddenly seems different or disappears from the market? It could be any product you have enjoyed using that suddenly, without warning, diminishes in quality. It could be a favorite paint that no longer covers the walls in one coat, a special cleaning product that no longer seems to take out cosmetic stains, or a jewelry cleaner that does not seem to make your diamond engagement ring sparkle like it used to. Or maybe the fabric of your favorite designer's new suit wrinkles abnormally or pills when worn. It could be any number of products that just do not provide the experience you were expecting.

Surely the founders of these companies did not present vision statements saying, "We will create a line of CD cases made of the thinnest plastic so that they break easily," or, "We will no longer make our customers our number-one priority. Instead, we will man our customer service department with rude and insensitive employees." Do you recall my complaint about the vanity mirror in my car? Surely the designer's worksheet did not state: "We will position the mirror on the sun visor of the driver's side so that the front seat passenger will have to lean far over in order to see herself." Chances are that it was caused by the gradual buildup of making one small cost-cutting measure after another. When cost-cutting impacts the quality of a product or service so deeply, it can jeopardize the entire business.

The Gibson guitar company of Nashville, Tennessee, is an excellent example of how an established business can lose its focus on quality and, even better, regain it. Gibson ranks as one of America's preeminent musical instrument manufacturers. Their fabulous guitars have been played through the years by famed guitarists such as Les Paul and Eric Clapton. Beginning in the 1960s, according to the company's current chief executive officer, Henry Juszkiewicz, management started buying and selling an enormously diversified portfolio of companies, from printing concerns to an Ecuadorian concrete company. Henry and his team bought the company in 1986. What they purchased, he says, "was a very sick company and a lot of things were wrong." For one thing, Henry says that Gibson had gotten into the practice of selling "seconds," "thirds," and even "fourths," instruments that did not meet the company's highest standards, as a way to compete with the many cheaper guitar imports in music stores.

Henry and his partners were determined to turn that scenario around. He studied and became an expert on the desires of musicians. He knew that in order to succeed, Gibson had to reclaim its former mantle as a fine-quality instrument maker. Henry feels strongly that to remain successful, a business must consistently produce good quality. "Somebody has actually got to care," he says. "It is an emotional involvement that creates success."

He proclaimed that Gibson would again stand for quality. He created a marketing campaign designed to position Gibson back at the top as a prestigious instrument maker. Henry continued, "I was not satisfied with the quality level or the commitment of the people in the factory to producing a quality product." To ensure that his craftsmen were truly building instruments worthy of Gibson's noble heritage, he announced to them that no second-rate musical instrument would ever leave the factory grounds again.

This was a dramatic initiative on his part. In another bold move, in one of his factories where guitars that did not meet the company's quality standards were stacked on top of one another waiting to be packaged and shipped to market, Henry instructed a craftsman, with everyone watching, to use a chainsaw to destroy every single one of those guitars. Henry certainly made an impression on his employees. From that moment on, it became a point of pride for his workers that their hard work should never suffer that fate again.

This dramatic event inspired a tremendous turnaround. During the next 15 years, Gibson realized a 30 percent compounded growth rate. In the last 5 years, they have enjoyed a growth rate of nearly 20 percent more. Gibson, with Henry Juszkiewicz at the helm, now sells about $300 million worth of the finest quality guitars, mandolins, and various other handcrafted instruments. Ironically, these days they actually have padlocks on their dumpsters. The Gibson name is so prestigious again that fans who dream of owning one of their guitars were raiding those dumpsters, hoping to find a discard or even a piece of a discarded guitar to collect. Remember Henry's decree? No second-rate musical instrument would ever leave the factory grounds again!

Quality must be part of your Big Idea

Don't misunderstand me. I am not saying that quality is so important that cost is insignificant. That, too, can be a recipe for failure. What I am suggesting is that quality must be in the forefront of your thoughts, even from the eureka moment when you first realize your Big Idea. Ensure that you can afford to accomplish what you intend to do in the highest quality way. Monitor how that goal is being met every day, in every way, in everything your company does. Unfortunately, for many companies, quality is the first thing to suffer when budgets become tight or competition makes it difficult to charge a price that will deliver a reasonable profit. But I remain insistent: Quality must be the last thing to be sacrificed!

If you are facing business challenges and are tempted to alter your quality, **don't!** Instead, take a hoe and pull out every extravagance, every excess, by its roots. Weed out every bit of waste in your company. If you throw money away on nonessential items, you are placing the quality of your products and thus your entire business at risk.

Once you have discarded the weeds and find that quality is still too hard to maintain, sit down, open your books, and really study to find out if you need to adapt your business to fit reality. For example, let us take a look at my friend, Melissa Neufeld. As you recall, several years ago, Melissa launched a wonderful paper craft business. She created lovely wrapping papers and cards out of extremely high-quality papers. Her products were a good value, but they were not inexpensive. Melissa wanted to make her products available to the mass market, so she did an analysis. What she discovered was that she could not afford to compete in the middle and low ends of the decorative paper business. Mass marketers had enormous economies of scale. She quickly understood that, as a small business, it would be impossible to sell her beautiful products at lower price levels. At the high end, however, she could offer upscale department stores and gift shops something unique for which higher-end customers would pay a premium, thus ensuring a reasonable profit. This was a smart, well-studied, realistic business decision. Melissa found a way to make a product whose quality pleased her and her customers and also made money.

She expanded by adding more products to her target market, not by trying to compete in an impossible segment of the market by using inferior-quality materials. Ultimately, her business grew into a thriving one.

Whatever you want to do with your business, do it in the highest quality way and then analyze the financial consequences of that decision. If the costs appear too daunting, look for manufacturing or retail partners or other innovative ways to share the costs, as Martha Stewart Living did with Kmart. If the numbers still do not look good, rethink the idea, then move in another direction.

Quality is not just about product development

The quest to balance quality and costs is a challenge for any business, large or small. It goes beyond actual product materials or ingredients into such areas as facilities and workforces. For example, I insist that my company workspaces are housed in buildings that have working windows so that fresh air can circulate. I want my employees to enjoy lots of natural light and clean, open spaces. I firmly believe that these basic, physical elements help to create an environment that is healthier and more conducive to creativity and productivity. Ultimately, albeit indirectly, a beautiful environment will affect the quality of our product. People are at their desks for 8 or more hours per day; they should not feel as though they have been sealed inside a stagnant, stale building exposed only to harsh, artificial light and recycled air.

My offices are located in Manhattan, one of the most expensive commercial real estate markets in the country. How do we get these particular quality features in our buildings? We make trade-offs. That does not mean that we use inferior photographers to take pictures for our publications or that we purchase cheap ingredients in our test kitchens. Instead, we have decided that health and comfort matters more than a prestigious or fancy address; we lease offices in areas that are undergoing a resurgence, where rents are less expensive and where we can afford to bring in talented architects to create the kinds of places we dream of: workable offices built simply from basic materials. There are few wall-to-wall carpets, no fancy veneers, no office suites of expensive furniture, and yet we now have three fabulous office/studio spaces in New York City: one on 42nd Street and two in the booming Chelsea district. The lure of a fancier address does not appeal to me if my employees are catching colds, breathing stale air all day, and never seeing sunlight.

Invest in your reputation

Let me end this chapter on quality by telling you about a young man who must often grapple with an unpredictable and volatile raw goods market as he strives to produce a superior product.

JOHN BARRICELLI
The priceless raspberry

From the very first time I sampled John Barricelli's mouth-watering desserts—his rich and creamy gelatos, his light and flaky pastries, his scrumptious and gorgeous cakes—I was convinced that John was a baker of great distinction. His great-grandfather came from Nola, Italy, and opened a bakery in Brooklyn around 1900. His grandfather followed in those footsteps, also working as a baker. Following family tradition, John attended the esteemed Culinary Institute of America in Hyde Park, New York. He later worked in such outstanding Manhattan restaurants as the Four Seasons and the Water Club. I met John in Connecticut when he was cooking at The Elms in Ridgefield. And that was a fortunate meeting because he later came to work for me at my television studio, baking, cooking, working with guest chefs, and managing the television prep kitchen. He is currently the tall, handsome man/chef on our **Everyday Food** show.

In addition to all of those impressive food credentials, John is an entrepreneur. Recently, he and another talented **Everyday Food** chef, Margot Olshan, opened the SoNo Baking Company and Café in Norwalk, Connecticut. This is John's third bakery and his largest, most ambitious endeavor to date. Not surprisingly, he is a fanatic when it comes to the quality of the ingredients he uses and the quality of the assistants he employs. After much hard labor, he and Margot have transformed the cavernous, raw space they leased into something grand and gorgeous. There is a comfortable, large seating area where customers can have coffee or tea and some tasty confection. There are baskets of artisanal breads baked several times a day, and the display cases are filled with an amazing selection of true masterpieces that can melt the most determined dieter's willpower.

Now that the bakery is up and running, John appreciates the challenge of holding true to good quality standards more than ever. "I get only the best ingredients—butter, chocolate, berries. If I am working with good chocolate, it's hard to make a bad chocolate cake," he explains. John agrees with me that "quality is a daily decision. The price of ingredients fluctuates. The butter I insist on using can go up and down 10 to 20 cents a pound; I can't be adjusting the price of a croissant 10 or 15 cents every day. But if I change butters, the croissants don't taste the same. If I pay $22 for a flat of raspberries, I make a small profit. If I have to pay $28, I only break even. Should I not use raspberries when they are expensive? If I think about how they look on the pastries in the showcase, the color, the rich look, I think they are priceless. It is worth it to have them there."

I find John's passion for quality inspiring. It even reminds me of facing similar challenges as a caterer when berry prices would shoot up. My solution was to place them in a ring around the outside of a pie or tart instead of using twice or three times that amount to cover the entire top of the dessert. That way, you had the look and color of the raspberries without losing money on the product.

I really hope you will heed this advice and make quality a core value of your company. If you do so, it will become one of the first questions you ask yourself when confronted with almost any business decision. It can be difficult, even painful, to accept that there are times when your commitment to quality will directly interfere with your profits. At MSLO, when we insist on good-quality paper for our magazine, we are cutting into our profits. When we test and refine recipes from scratch in our kitchens, we are investing money others might not spend. When we hire the best, not the cheapest talent available, we are investing in our reputation and our future.

Find a way to function frugally in every aspect of your business while not affecting your customers or hurting your employees. Do not pare down your customers' experience if you can possibly avoid it. Over time, your avid devotion to quality will set you apart. It will so pervade your company's business and reputation that short-term losses will be offset by loyal customers who fuel your long-term growth. I understand and know something about customer loyalty. The many letters we have received from our readers and viewers describing how much the quality of our magazine and products has meant to them tell me that I made the right decision in maintaining and guarding quality in all our efforts through the years.

Fortunately for the SoNo Baking Company and Café, the future already looks bright. On a recent Sunday morning, just a few weeks after their opening, John and Margot served brunch to more than 130 sit-down customers. They had more than 600 walk-in customers, including the mayor of Norwalk, who purchased buttery croissants and those luscious berry tarts. My mouth is watering. I'll have to get back there soon, myself, and have a cappuccino and a cannoli. Yum!

Build an A-team

Martha's Rule

7

SEEK OUT AND HIRE EMPLOYEES WHO ARE
BRIMMING WITH TALENT, ENERGY,
INTEGRITY, OPTIMISM, AND GENEROSITY.
SEARCH FOR ADVISORS AND PARTNERS WHO
COMPLEMENT YOUR SKILLS AND
UNDERSTAND YOUR IDEALS.

WHEN YOUR BUSINESS PLAN IS FORMULATED
and you are ready to take on the world, it is
of utmost importance to hire the right team
players in order to win. As an entrepreneur,
it is most gratifying to watch a group of intelligent, talented people be transformed
from employees working for a paycheck into

an energetic staff that collaborates day into night to achieve a common goal, knowing that they fully understand and respectfully embrace the love and passion that you have for your Big Idea, your business.

As I write this chapter, naturally, I turn my thoughts to my own wonderful staff and to a few individuals in particular whom I have hired throughout the years who have made an enormous difference. When I think and write about these people, my mood becomes elevated. It makes me genuinely happy to remember all the amazing contributions they have made for the betterment of the company. I am most fortunate to have met Gael Towey many years ago. As our first art director, Gael was largely responsible for creating the unique look and design of the magazine, for which she and the company have received many awards. Now, as creative director, Gael oversees the design of thousands of innovative, functional, highly attractive, and useful products for our valued customers, all packaged in evermore striking ways. Margaret Roach joined me first as my gardening editor and has now been my editor in chief for almost a decade. Every time I read one of Margaret Roach's spirited commentaries—"One potato, two potato, three potato, four. Or better yet, a hundred. I want to see, touch, grow, taste—and document—them all"—I think of Margaret's enthusiasm and how her talents have transformed **Martha Stewart Living.**

For so many others, like editorial director of decorating Kevin Sharkey, for example, or editorial director of collecting Fritz Karch, it feels so good and natural to be around them, that it is difficult to remember how we met in the first place. Kevin has an astonishing sense of style and design. He has helped me decorate all of my homes. He is someone who can talk and talk about color, fabrics, and design, but he also loves to fill vases full of beautiful flowers, go antiquing, and climb the hills of Acadia with me and my other friends. Fritz understands my passion for antiques and collectibles. He is constantly bringing new ideas to the business that always seem to create a stir in the marketplace, and he constantly reminds us to revere the vintage past and distinguish this antique from that. Eric Pike, a creative director, oversees the publications' designs and works on all of the books we publish. His uncanny talent for clean, evocative design and his love for purity in all creative aspects of his work never cease to please and astonish me and our colleagues.

There are many other employees who have been with us almost since the beginning, who have made and continue to make valuable contributions to our company, people such as Dora Cardinale, who is in charge of print production, and Lauren Stanich, who heads publishing. I consider employees such as these to be fine examples of my A-team. It delights me that they choose to share their time and their treasured talents with me and my company. I have an especially big smile for Darcy Miller, who came to MSLO in 1992 as a young, temporary worker. When I met her, I knew right away that her temporary status was just that. Darcy possessed that certain "something" that was hard for anyone to miss. Today, she is editor in chief of our magazine, **Martha Stewart Weddings.** Her own fabulous wedding was historically captured in the pages of that publication. As an invited guest, I was instructed to observe, as silently as I could (after all, Darcy is also an expert on weddings), both the meticulous preparations and the day itself—absolutely perfect and exactly what I would have wished for this motivated, driven, and talented young woman. After all, I did introduce her to her husband! These are only a handful of my valued employees, and I really could go on, making this book a whole lot thicker. However, I think my point is clear about seeking and hiring only the best.

Good employees will energize you and your business

As I have stated, I feel very fortunate because my life and my work are interchangeable; and because both are so intertwined, I get to spend quite a bit of time outside official work hours with employees and business associates who are interesting and witty and just plain fun to be around. Susan Magrino, my long-time public relations consultant, fits into this category. I remember fondly the trip around the country we took together when we were promoting **Entertaining.** Promotion is essential for sales, but such an extended trip—about 3 weeks—is grueling. Because you are on a rigid schedule, the talks you give and the cities you visit start blurring together. By the time we reached California, Susan could tell that I needed a break from the grind. She provided the perfect antidote. She pulled up to our luxurious hotel entrance in a rented turquoise Cadillac convertible, and we proceeded to drive up the coast from Los Angeles to Monterey, stopping along the route for refreshments and visits with friends. Susan shares my appreciation for great food, and she arranged this leg of the trip so that we would stop at two or three celebrated restaurants each day to sample delicious local cuisine along the way. Wearing head scarves and business attire and using the **Zagat** guide as a roadmap, we hardworking girls had a fantastic publicity tour. Susan turned what could have been an exhausting trip into an exciting and mouthwatering adventure, and the book did get on the bestseller list.

I am proud of most of my employees, but I must admit that I have had my share of hiring errors. There have been some difficult partings and unsuccessful collaborations. It makes me very unhappy to come to the realization that the wrong person was hired for a particular job, even though that person was smart and talented and promising. On the other hand, I know we all make mistakes and that an unhappy employee, someone who is in the wrong position, for example, can be quite damaging to the company. Friction results from constant complaining and can undermine the positive feelings of fellow employees, and negative energy can create paranoia. Job insecurity can lead to poor decision-making. And because unhappy people do not make good team players, they cannot have respect for your ideals and your goals. Terminating an unsuccessful hire is painful for both the particular employee and the unhappy employer. A swift action, fairly carried out, is best for all. That is certainly a key premise of my television show, **The Apprentice: Martha Stewart,** where in every segment someone was selected to depart because they just didn't fit in. While the contestants on the show came from widely varying backgrounds and made a range of different mistakes, those asked to leave generally had two things in common: They misread what the customer wanted and needed, and they just didn't work hard enough.

If you are prudent, however, and carefully hire the right people, those employees will make all the difference in both your confidence level and your success. They will energize your business and make every day rewarding and enjoyable. They will know what you expect and will even get work done without your having to ask. And because they understand exactly what the business means to you, they will be happy and proud doing the work they were hired to do.

To partner or not to partner

Before I discuss those considerations that are essential when hiring, I would like to discuss two groups of people who are not employees per se, but rather people you choose to work with who can help you steer toward success. These are partners and consultants/advisors.

Many entrepreneurs enter into business with a partner. A silent partner may simply contribute financial resources to the effort, while a more active partner may have different skills than yours and will actually invest "sweat equity," just as you do. In a real estate development business, for example, one partner may be outstanding at finding properties, determining what is required to add value, and later marketing that value. The other may be a hands-on builder who organizes the job, obtains the permits, assembles the crew, and manages the projects. In a small, craft-based enterprise, one person may deal with design and the production of the product, while another partner handles marketing and sales.

But there is another significant advantage in having a partner—the psychological support of knowing that you are not alone in trying to make something difficult work. No matter how much passion you have for the business you are building, on any given day the unexpected can and will occur. It may be as serious as a death in the family, a medical emergency for yourself, the fact that your child-care person could not come to work, or some other problem that needs your undivided attention. When everything rests on your shoulders alone, facing events such as these can overwhelm you to the point where you may wonder, "What was I thinking? With such distractions, this business idea will never work!" It is precisely because of moments like these that a good partner is welcome. How wonderful if someone were to say, "Please, take the day off. You obviously need it. I can handle things while you are gone. Call, let me know how things are going, but don't feel you need to come back until things are settled. Everything will be okay!"

Unfortunately, many entrepreneurial partnerships are formed because friends with similar interests decide it would be a good idea to work together. You may have a strong bond in friendship, but that bond is not sufficient to ensure a strong partnership. Determining whether a partnership will work involves asking serious questions: What does each of us bring to this endeavor, and are they equal in value? Are our skills complementary? Will we share fairly in all aspects of the business, or will one of us want to work only on the enjoyable aspects? Are we in agreement about division of labor, ownership in the enterprise, reinvestment of profits in the business, as well as in our ultimate goals for the business? Do not take a partner until questions like these are answered.

Ponder these questions slowly and deliberately. It is important to put your emotions aside and be both realistic and objective. Every potential partnership is different, and it is true that there are some very unlikely pairings that have gone on to produce some extraordinary companies and businesses. There are, of course, many examples of hideous fallings-out that have destroyed both the friendships and the enterprise itself. At Martha Stewart Living, I have always been the primary "owner" and visionary. However, I consider several of the "founding" employees to be partners. There have been other employees, too, who have made invaluable contributions to the success of the company. Some of these have left, but they were very well compensated and treated like minority partners with "ownership" while they were making their contributions to Martha Stewart Living Omnimedia.

Beware the echo chamber: assembling an advisory board

Your advisors, both formal and informal, can be the other essential members of your business life. Formal advisors include people such as your accountants and attorneys— professionals having skills far too complicated and expensive to develop adequately yourself when you are in the midst of starting a business. You must adopt a process every bit as rigorous as hiring an employee when interviewing and hiring professional consultants; and you should diligently follow up on the references they give you, paying particular attention to clients with businesses similar in scope to your own. Later, when you realize a certain level of success, you may want to or have to create a formal board of directors for your company, as we have done at MSLO. A board is comprised of individuals who are compensated, in a formally agreed-upon manner, and who meet periodically to advise you and your company, based on their areas of expertise or experience.

In a small business, I believe it is essential to assemble an informal advisory team from the earliest days of operation. It is fine to have the support and wishful thinking from your family and friends, but you need other, experienced people who can offer advice based on actual, practical knowledge. Without engaging such counsel, many would-be entrepreneurs have failed. Remember that contracts need to be formalized, that financial reports have to be prepared in a timely and accurate way, and that banks require excellent accounting procedures even for a small loan. Because there are so many disparate elements that comprise MSLO, we have gathered an extensive network of business advisors as well as personal friends and mentors in specific fields. We are always seeking counsel and listening to the advice they give us.

You may be wondering where you find such people and why they would be willing to devote their time to help you out. I have already mentioned why mentors are so important. If you stand out as a hard worker who is an expert in your field, you stand a great chance of collecting mentors who recognize bits of themselves in your bubbling pride and enthusiasm. People like that are simply honored to help you. But also keep in mind that various suppliers and businesspeople you associate with can be patched into your advisor network. This network is kind of like a patchwork security blanket. Use it and find comfort there. I remember when I was preparing to purchase my company from Time Inc. I and some of my "mentoring friends" had regular, weekly planning meetings around my kitchen table in East Hampton, where lively conversations took place about all aspects of such a business move. I could never have accomplished such a feat without the help and advice of those friends.

Joelle Hoverson happened upon some valuable advisors for her knitting shop in the wholesale companies from which she acquired wool. For any retailer, wholesale suppliers can be very good sources of information on current trends in the marketplace. They can provide tips on what other retailers are doing and trying, and they have some perspective on what is working or not. The reps from Joelle's wholesalers were thrilled to see another outlet opening, one that would require their supplies. This made them quite happy to spend extra time with a budding retailer, discussing products and marketing ideas. And yet, although Joelle was glad for the help, she would be the first to tell you that you have to take some of this advice with a grain of salt. For example, a company may have invested in a certain kind of product that is not catching on. The retailer must rely on his or her own judgment about whether a sales rep's enthusiasm can be trusted or if the rep is just trying to push a slow-selling item.

Most businesses develop mutually beneficial interests with other businesses that can create productive relationships and conversations for each. Wedding planners, caterers, and floral designers; sporting goods stores and personal trainers; restaurants and hotels share mutual interests. Every town has a Chamber of Commerce, and every industry has a lobbying and trade association. There are professional associations for everything you can imagine, from apple growers to interior designers, musicians to physical therapists, resort owners to zookeepers. It is far easier to build a network than you might think. The Internet makes these matchmakings easier than it has ever been simply by providing names and information with a few clicks of a mouse.

A word of caution: Be smart in how you approach potential advisors. Be assertive when asking for their help, but keep in mind that it is the nature of human interaction that others will expect something from you in return. Look for ways that you can benefit from the association while keeping all business arrangements as clear and as professional as possible.

Hiring the right person

John Barricelli's new bakery in Norwalk, Connecticut, is a smashing success. Yet if you ask him about the major challenges he faces, he becomes downright somber when he explains how difficult it is to find good workers. I happened to call him one day immediately after an excellent employee, who he thought would have a long future with his business, called and quit without warning. "Hiring is the most disheartening part of the business for me," John says.

John is not alone. I know many people who feel this way, even in large companies. I consider myself fortunate that throughout my career I was able to hire so many outstanding people to fill so many interesting jobs. There have been some mistakes, and I have found that it is best to remedy the situation via a parting of ways rather than to hope the situation will somehow get better.

At MSLO, when we hire anyone new, we are especially meticulous and proceed with great caution, and that has paid off. Recently, however, I have reflected quite a bit on the hiring challenge we faced during the making of **The Apprentice: Martha Stewart.** If you had the luxury of requiring every job candidate to try out by working on different teams doing seven high-intensity tasks over a 10-week period, you would make very few mistakes when hiring. On the show, it was fascinating to observe the candidates' true personalities emerge, sometimes surprising us pleasantly, other times not so pleasantly. The ancient practice of having a true apprentice is a wise one that I wish was more practical to reinstate today. The notion of a trial period of work, to observe productivity, personality, and the ability of the apprentice to function in the business environment you have created, or of hiring that applicant as a consultant before hiring him or her as an employee, is also a good idea.

Hiring employees presents a dilemma. There have been extremely qualified candidates from whom I have felt energy, creativity, and enthusiasm but who ultimately did not make effective employees in our particular environment. What did we miss? How did we make these hiring mistakes? What can you do to avoid making similar errors?

There are some well-understood and yet often ignored rules that can help you as you embark on the path of recruiting appropriate and reliable employees. In most cases, they apply equally well to entry-level employees and to executives. These are very basic guidelines, but many hiring problems are the result of not doing these things correctly. Perhaps the most fundamental mistake we make as employers is making an emotional decision instead of a rational one.

1.
CREATE OPTIONS BY CONSIDERING SEVERAL CANDIDATES.

Never hire the first person who walks in the door, no matter how talented and perfect the person appears, without considering a couple of other candidates for that job. This is especially important in a small start-up business. Understand that you may just be inflating that person's suitability because you desperately need the help! This is when it is essential to use your informal network. Spread the word among your mentors, professional advisors, suppliers, friends, and family that you are hiring. In addition, post help-wanted ads in the usual places. Always request a resumé from each applicant, and insist on references! Make a list of attributes the ideal employee for that job should have, and compare that list with the qualities present in your pool of candidates. Do not be discouraged if a "perfect" candidate does not emerge right off the bat. Instead, think seriously about the most important attributes you're looking for and how you can help that person who displays the most promise fill in any gaps. This exercise, alone, will not only help you hire better people but will force you to think about what you really want and need for your business.

2 .
CHECK THOSE REFERENCES!

There are people, sad to say, who can spin quite a tale of accomplishment and competence in a job interview but who sometimes are unable to satisfy the most minimal aspects of their job. Beware of too much overt enthusiasm and effusiveness. You are looking for evidence of a good work ethic, good judgment, and high standards. These are things you absolutely must investigate by following up on a job candidate's references. Ask former employers: Is this person reliable? What kind of attitude and personality does this person demonstrate on the job? What are this person's strengths and weaknesses? Does the person's experience match up with what he or she really did while working for you?

People sometimes go an amazingly long way in business before an employer discovers that they have inflated or fabricated their educational level or early job experience. Remember that even checking references is not a foolproof method. The current liability climate discourages some former employers from being negative or critical of former employees' performances. However, you can generally infer, even from the reference source's tone and style of answering, just how valuable the employee was. I will again refer to the candidates on **The Apprentice: Martha Stewart.** I was shocked at the behavior and attitudes of some of the candidates outside of my presence. Seeing them away from the tasks, away from the conference room, behind the scenes, was proof enough that they really did not have the physical and/or moral fiber necessary to work in our environment.

3 .
MAKE SURE ALL INVOLVED EMPLOYEES
MEET THE CANDIDATE.

There is an expression in business that some people "manage up" very well, but they do not prove to be team players or good leaders. This means that they invest a lot of time in positioning themselves with their own managers and much less time than they should doing the hard work of their own jobs, even to the point of being dismissive or abrasive to their staffs. If you make certain that every candidate meets the people with whom he or she will be working, it will be clear from the beginning that the individual is joining a team where everyone's opinion matters. When your employees describe to the job candidate the actual work of the job, those people may pick up positive or negative clues to the applicant's personality, training, or intentions that will be important factors when making your decision. Be open to and respectful of your team's suggestions. You do not want them to resent the person you finally hire, as the team may find a way to make sure that person does not succeed.

Clearly, there is a very good reason why most companies add human-resource professionals to the mix as the company grows. There is an art and a science to hiring and managing people, and what I have given you are just some very basic rules. Unfortunately, like many basic rules, they are often overlooked in the heady yet frantic early days of a small business.

Cutting through the purple haze

As you hire new employees, spend some time with them, and be quite specific as to what you expect from them. Guidance is all important. Get to know their personalities, paying particular attention to things that seem even slightly odd. Truly bizarre events can arise over incorrect assumptions. For example, for many years my magazine staff was under the impression that I disliked the color purple. Although not my favorite color, I have never disliked purple of any shade. I loved reading the book **The Color Purple,** and I especially loved the movie. I think of purple as a seasonal color; I adore my purple pansies, my fragrant lilacs, Concord grapes, and lavender plants. So why did they think I was adverse to purple? As it turns out, the magazine printed a story once on flower arranging. One particular layout featured an arrangement in a purple vase, and I thought the entire layout was unattractive and said as much. Apparently my comment was too general of a statement or it was misunderstood, because my editors assumed I disliked purple, and consequently our readers were denied purple for years.

This was hardly a tragic offense, but it caused me to take heed. A company founder must be aware that even an offhand comment can have far-reaching effects. This is a common problem throughout an organization, even among experienced employees. However, a new, insecure employee can be thrown way off track from a simple misconception and never feel comfortable to openly ask an executive to clarify. Constantly reiterate, even with small, occasional utterances, what exactly your philosophy and values are to all of your employees. In fact, I make it a point to become personally involved in the development of talented people in the company. I see how they are doing: I go to photo shoots, on sales calls, and out into the field. I view these as important opportunities to share my thought process and to help good employees become great.

We are now in the process of creating a book describing our design philosophy at Martha Stewart Living. Although I know the book will be an invaluable text for design schools and graphic arts courses everywhere, it will be most valuable for the scores of new employees who enter the workforce at our company, for it will very clearly and lucidly inform them and teach them and remind them of what our company is trying to do every day.

Truly constructive criticism

When it comes to managing, I follow my instincts. I listen and gather advice, but I take responsibility for what my educated instincts tell me about what needs to be done—about strategy, about direction, about people. This is what life is like for an entrepreneur. An entrepreneur takes responsibility for a vision and does what he or she can to make it work.

One somewhat controversial management technique that I do believe in is critiquing our products internally, all the time. We have always critiqued every issue of **Martha Stewart Living,** and I honestly believe that my team looks forward to these sessions. It is highly important to them that we continually improve and are careful not to repeat mistakes. Only by openly discussing what is working or not working can the team consistently improve. A number of my executives have questioned that approach. They feel that, in these sessions, certain employees get discouraged or have their feelings hurt. My argument to them is that the more frequently these open discussions take place, the easier it is to evaluate the business culture. I know that I am harder on myself than I have ever been on my employees. I believe that is the backbone for creating high standards and, even more important, changing when you need to change. Your employees need leadership to keep improving and keep hitting newer and higher marks. If you are resistant to change or if you refuse to change, you may as well call it a day. In other words, when you are through changing, you're through.

The right people for the right time

Even if you follow all of this advice precisely, you will still find that people are complex, changing organisms and that what worked well last month may suddenly not be working at all. Just when a team seems to be perfectly balanced and working harmoniously, a spouse may be transferred to another state, and there goes your best manager. The next person in line may not be ready for the responsibility. Or two employees may begin wrangling, and no amount of persuasion can restore the trust so vital to the team's production. Or perhaps your best salesperson suddenly encounters a new buyer at your biggest customer and that relationship becomes rocky. Entrepreneurs must accept the reality that some people are right for a business at a particular time, but if business needs change and the people do not, it is time to make a change. That change could mean offering an employee a different job within your company if you are growing rapidly, or the employee may need to move on to a new opportunity somewhere else. You must accept this fact at the start and brace yourself for the tough decisions that this reality requires.

We are long past the days when the goal of a business was to provide what used to be called lifetime employment. It is absolutely imperative to impress that philosophy upon your employees from day one. The message should be: We are a growing, learning, and vibrant organization. We invite you to grow and learn with us, but we will always organize our business around the people we believe are necessary to accomplish our next goal. We dream of creating perfect teams and keeping everyone happy forever, but that is not likely to happen. At least we will all be as honest and open with each other as we possibly can so that there are no surprises.

This should not sound like a threat. Rather, you should explain that you are simply laying out the rules for the kind of company you intend to build. It does no one any good to hold on to an ineffective employee. It can only hurt your business and all the good people working for you.

The monkey-wrench factor

People can get stale in certain kinds of jobs, while others find ways to reinvent their own jobs and challenge themselves to do things better all the time. After 12 years of taping my daily television show, I was tired of the format and knew I was ready for a change. I felt the team I had could grow in new directions. That is why the thought of working on a live show with Mark Burnett was so exciting for me. It is such a change and one some of my colleagues could not grasp. But as I begin our first season, I am really looking forward to forging into new territory and creating new content.

A good manager will notice if an employee appears to be feeling stale or uninspired and will offer that person a new challenge. I call it tossing a monkey wrench into the works. I have had the most wonderful experiences encouraging people to try something completely new and different—something I know they are already interested in. Gael Towey, my creative director, calls this "putting people in stretch roles," and we have stretched so many wonderful people into exciting new jobs. Eric Pike, our executive creative director, came on board as a graphic designer and evolved into a true executive having a much broader vision and a very good business sense. Because of that, Eric has stretched quite nicely into one of the top jobs in our company.

Always searching for new synergistic businesses means that you can help your employees use their experience in new ways to keep their energy levels high and their interests keen. MSLO is currently moving into the satellite radio business, and that has sent sparks flying through the entire company as staff members come up with ideas for interesting new programs for our radio channel.

Some management experts recommend that people should professionally "repot" themselves at least every 10 years. As a gardener, I can relate to that! We all tend to bury our roots deep into our personal situations, becoming stale and stubborn, often to our detriment. If you find a valued employee becoming a bit stale and stubborn, encourage him or her to "repot," to develop new talents and branch out.

An unusual source of satisfaction

Recently, I received an e-mail from Susan Hanneman, a senior associate food editor at **Everyday Food** magazine. After reading it, I thought, "How nice! How great! How sad!"

Susan was looking for a letter of recommendation because she was applying to business schools. She is a Tufts graduate and an award-winning chef with a degree from Kendall Culinary College. Susan was executive chef in her own restaurant in Memphis, Tennessee, and I vividly recall the time she was a guest on my television show and prepared an aromatic and succulent bourbon-glazed ham. She is absolutely passionate about the food business, and she has a wonderful job at my company, where her work is highly valued. You might be wondering why I would feel happy to lose such an important asset. It's because I have learned that a smart businessperson should always value talent and should always be pleased when an employee wishes to develop in important and positive ways—even if it means letting go of that person. I have so many terrific friends, many of whom were once my employees. Because I am a teacher, this is a source of great pride and satisfaction for me, knowing that their experience with me and my company was productive for us both and enabled them to go off and realize their own dreams.

Like most successful people, Susan is bright, well organized, and does a lot of research and talking to experts before she makes a move. This is what drew her to my company in the first place. After running a successful restaurant with her family, Susan wanted to try out the world of food publishing. She interviewed with all the food publications in New York City. When she finally came to us, it was clear that she would be a perfect fit in our kitchens, first for **Martha Stewart Living** and later for **Everyday Food.** Susan now realizes that, with a business degree, she can complement her already strong skills and take herself in exciting new directions within the food industry. "I want to make a substantial professional leap," Susan says, "but there are some skills I don't have. I've got an entrepreneur's spirit, but the business degree is the missing puzzle piece." In a later chapter, I will explain the importance of investing in yourself and your business at key times, and Susan is a perfect example of that. She is passionate and an expert in her field; she has a good reputation; and soon she will have the kind of education that will enable her to choose from a broad array of options.

I feel completely confident that our paths will cross again. Susan may someday run my food business or launch something even more exciting that neither one of us can yet imagine. You should be envious of the exciting journey on which Susan is about to embark, because I so believe in the power, joy, and value of lifelong learning. When you are through changing, you're through!

By the way, Susan did get accepted to the MIT Sloan School of Management for the 2006 entering class.

So the pie isn't perfect? Cut it into wedges

Martha's Rule 8

WHEN FACED WITH A BUSINESS CHALLENGE,
EVALUATE OR ASSESS THE SITUATION,
GATHER THE GOOD THINGS IN SIGHT,
ABANDON THE BAD, CLEAR YOUR MIND, AND
MOVE ON. FOCUS ON THE POSITIVE. STAY
IN CONTROL, AND NEVER PANIC.

BACK IN MY CATERING DAYS, I was fortunate to have many wonderful repeat customers, and some of my clients were well-known celebrities. When I was hired to cater a dinner for my fellow Westporters, Paul Newman and Joanne Woodward, I almost had to pinch myself. Not long before this booking, I had taken a driving tour of Morocco with my husband. Morocco was a feast for the eyes: craggy mountains, endless deserts, and miles of snow white, flowering almond orchards. Morocco was also a feast for the palate. I sampled the most incredible stews, called tagines, bursting with flavors both sweet and savory. The tagines were served over pale yellow mounds of steaming couscous. I was served a pigeon pie, called b'steeya, the savory contents encased in the flakiest pastry. Its flavors were deep and exotic. I thought this cuisine would make extraordinary party fare. At the bustling markets, I bartered for spices, canned condiments, and the necessary implements to prepare these dishes, including special copper couscous steamers and the heavy, terracotta-colored two-part clay tagines. We returned home with suitcases bulging and laps piled high with heavy pots.

When the Newmans called for a consultation, I was well prepared with a unique idea, and they were enchanted with the concept of a Moroccan buffet. I described the huge platters and colorful dishes, and they hired me to recreate many of the dishes I had sampled, including eight b'steeya, four made with chicken and the others with squab, which was more like the pigeon I had eaten in Marrakesh. Just a few hours before the party, I put the prepared b'steeya into the preheated oven. During baking, they looked just fine to me, and then I made the fatal error of getting distracted and leaving the kitchen. When I removed the b'steeya from the oven, I was horrified to see that each pie had a very badly burned crust on that portion of the pie that had been closest to the oven wall. (Now I make it a rule never to leave anything cooking without taking a timer in my pocket. When cooking shrimp, I do not even leave the stove.)

The pies, one of three main courses, were central to the buffet. My mind was full of horrifying visions. My reputation as a caterer was at stake. The pies were time-consuming to prepare, and it would be impossible to recreate them. I took a deep breath and made an assessment. I saw that although the pies were no longer perfect, the vast majority of each was fine and undamaged. I picked up a serrated knife, cut each pie into wedges, discarded the damaged portions, gathered the perfect pieces, sprinkled them with crisscrosses of powdered sugar and cinnamon, arranged them on huge brass trays, took them to the party, and served them. I acted as though nothing were amiss, and the party was a huge success. I never breathed a word of this to the Newmans or to anyone else, for that matter. I did what had to be done. The pies, now in wedges, were utterly delicious. Problem solved. Sorry, Joanne and Paul, but you may not have understood at the time.

From Kilimanjaro to Alderson

I always smile at the memory of that day. After all, if every party, every idea, every business venture succeeded without unexpected setbacks and the occasional threat of disaster, the world would be a rather boring place. Getting over these unexpected hurdles may not be exactly enjoyable, but ultimately I believe that such challenges and the solutions we find give us more confidence. They teach us that, with common sense and determination, we can turn what looks like a disaster into a triumph.

Never in my wildest dreams did I imagine that I would draw on the basic lessons of this Moroccan party to help me endure something far more critical. From early 2002 through 2005, I was involved in a protracted and exhausting legal battle. I was encouraged by my board of directors and attorneys to resign as CEO and chairwoman of the company I had started, the company that still bears my name. This was despite the fact that the legal issues were in no way related to my activities as a corporate officer. Ultimately, I was sentenced to a 5-month term in Alderson and another 5 months under home confinement.

During the long months of investigation and the trial and while waiting for the sentencing to occur, I awoke each day hoping that I was only having a really bad dream. I had spent my career and built my company's reputation working hard to bring Good

Things to as many people as possible. And yet a personal stock trade was threatening to destroy everything: my successful television show, my much-loved magazine and book projects, a nationally syndicated radio show, a vibrant product design and merchandising business, and a highly creative staff that was never at a loss for ideas. Wall Street valued us, our growth was good, and our prospects were extremely bright.

When the press broke the story that the government was investigating me, so much changed. Media coverage became increasingly negative, horrible rumors spread, and the stock of my valued company plummeted. But one thing remained constant. From day one of this horrible nightmare, I received enormous numbers of letters and e-mails—supportive, positive messages from my viewers, readers, listeners, and customers. Partners such as Kmart stood firmly behind my company.

I remember all too well the weariness, frustration, and the surreal quality of those days. Nearly a decade before, I had experienced something akin to those feelings on a trek up Mount Kilimanjaro. On the last day of the journey, our small party departed our camp at Kibo hut a few minutes after midnight. The strategy was to make it to the summit before dawn to watch the sun rise over magnificent Africa. The climb was exhausting, and with the peak in sight, the group had split into two. One guide led my two fellow climbers, and the other paired off with me. At 19,000 feet, with the oxygen so thin that it was difficult to breathe, my guide suddenly became ill. His nose was bleeding from the effects of the high altitude, and it was imperative that he descend. I weighed the choices: to proceed alone or return with him, as he advised, and miss my chance at the summit. I could not fathom the idea of turning back without having reached the top, but I was also aware that I was on a dangerous trail, that I was physically exhausted and feeling light-headed, even giddy in the thin air. There were no guarantees that I could catch up to the lead group or even finish the climb. Plus, if something went wrong, I would have to resolve the problem myself. I trudged on, determined, eating snow to keep myself going (my guide had forgotten to bring water or food, an indication that he was indeed ill before we began our ascent) and breathing deeply and slowly in the very thin air. The apex, after all, was in sight. I climbed, step after treacherous step, but I made it just in time to witness the first rays of sunlight illuminating that part of the continent. I had followed my instincts and persevered.

Over the course of the legal investigation and the trial that followed, I felt many of the same physical sensations. I was exhausted, barely sleeping, and worried constantly about the future of my company and my employees. My executives were facing intense pressure to disassociate the company from me. They looked to me for assurance, which I tried to give, but the legal snows grew ever deeper.

What's in a name?

At my lowest point, just before conviction, I was pondering something that today seems utterly ridiculous. "Maybe I should change my name," I actually thought. "Maybe I can protect my company and my wonderful employees by distancing myself from the brand. If I become Martha Kostyra again, maybe then people can separate this personal matter from the value and worth of my company." This actually seemed like a real solution to me at the time.

I have already mentioned how the enormous support of my customers and fans and those hundreds of thousands of e-mails and letters helped to lift my spirits. But the verdict, when it was finally read aloud on March 4, 2004, was sad and discouraging for me, as was the judge's sentence, handed down a few months later.

Just as with my b'steeya mishap, it was time for me to fully evaluate the situation, cut the pie into wedges, gather the good parts, and move on. My lawyers were adamant that we would appeal; and, of course, I was in full agreement. However, there was simply no telling how long an appeal would take. It could very well drag on and on and on, and in the end, I might go to prison anyway. In order to save my company from irreparable harm, I knew it was time to slice my situation into wedges.

I realized that it would be in everyone's best interests for me to complete my prison term and home confinement, even as my lawyers aggressively pursued my appeal. I had built a great company, but that company had been battered—and yet I firmly believed it could weather this terrible storm. The company's good, solid core was intact—an enormous library of valuable information, a powerful brand identity, and an outstanding and creative staff. We had millions of loyal fans who were still buying our products, still reading our magazines, and still eager for us to introduce them to a myriad of useful, beautiful things. Those realizations gave me strength and courage to make the preparations that I hoped would put the crippling, toxic uncertainty far behind all of us.

I had a lot of work to do to get ready for my term of incarceration. Each piece of the pie had to be in order. Many parts of my personal life had to be attended to. When I flew off to the facility, I felt confident that many things could proceed without me because the correct wheels had been set in motion.

I must tell you that, although my stay at Alderson had none of the fun and spice of a Moroccan buffet, it was a far better experience than I had anticipated. It is no secret that I am accustomed to being in control—of my life and of my company. What became all too apparent during my confinement was how many, many women are not in control of their lives or what happens to them. They endure extraordinarily difficult situations, yet remain very strong, nonetheless, both physically and emotionally. I made it a priority to really try to understand my fellow inmates, and they did the same for me. They were so curious about my business and how and why I had accomplished so much. One group, who were followers of the Muslim faith, asked permission to have me speak at a forum about business practices, and I was allowed to do so. It was gratifying to share ideas—everything from how to develop a Big Idea to the ins and outs of Internet advertising. They were so grateful, so warm, and so excited to have answers to their questions. In fact this book began there, at Alderson, with my preparation for that business seminar.

When I was released from prison, draped in a beautifully crocheted poncho from my friend and fellow inmate, Xiomara Hernandez, I knew it was time to assess my life again. During my stay, I had been so fortunate to have a steady stream of family and friends who visited me. Believe me, many women in prison are visited by no one for years. There were many things that I had missed—my animals, my homes, fresh food, travel, and the daily challenges of managing an endlessly interesting business. But there were just as many wonderful things that I had gathered during those 5 months—new friendships, so many ideas, and so much information and knowledge from fascinating books that I actually had the time to read. I also gained a new appreciation for the complexity of every single person's situation. I even emerged with a funny and memorable new nickname: M. Diddy. Despite the reality of the situation, good humor prevailed at Alderson.

Detours are part of the journey

It is important to be realistic and to always remember that no matter how high you set your standards, no matter how intense your devotion to quality, no matter how detailed your business plan, stuff—I choose to use the more polite **S** word here—will happen. Great employees will quit; competitors will appear out of nowhere; critics will disparage you unfairly; fire will rage through your warehouse; investors will want you to go in one direction while you want to go in another. Perhaps a hurricane will ravage your state and destroy what you have built. Or perhaps your confidence will simply waiver when too many little problems mount up together.

As an entrepreneur, be prepared for these occasional dark nights and remain steadfast. However bleak things may at first appear, if you are a good person doing things for the right reason, there is always something to grasp onto to help you carry on or start over again. There is no entrepreneur, anywhere, whose journey is without setbacks and crossroads. Take a look at my very dear and funny friend, the petkeeper Marc Morrone.

MARC MORRONE
Flying above adversity

I first met Marc in 1997. While staying at my home on Long Island, I tuned into a local cable television channel, and there was this Dr. Doolittle type chattering pleasantly and intelligently about animals, specifically pets. A colorful parrot named Harry was perched on his shoulder, tugging on his glasses with its enormous beak. The table before him was covered with all sorts of animals—feathered, scaly, and furry—all getting along perfectly well. Marc introduced each one by name and explained its characteristics. As you know, I love animals, and I was mesmerized. Marc clearly had a real gift for communicating with his pets, and I wanted him on my show. I called Marc the next morning at 8, and he and his menagerie became regular guests. Today, he is one of our stars, with columns in two of our magazines and a weekly show called **Petkeeping with Marc Morrone.**

Marc is one of those passionate entrepreneurs to whom I always enjoy talking. He is a creative thinker; and no matter what kinds of challenges he faces, he always finds a way to prevail. He does not panic, and he does not complain. Instead, he sets out to find a solution.

Marc opened his pet store, called Parrots of the World, in 1978 in Rockville Center, Long Island. Specializing in exotic birds imported from tropical climates, his business was soon thriving. The animal import business has had many difficulties, including smuggling, endangered species investigations, customs problems, tariffs, and more. There have been some very unethical people involved in that world who have been notorious for abusing and neglecting the animals they have sold. Unfortunately for humane dealers like Marc, the US government acted to stop the abuses by banning the import of parrots and other exotic birds, which had been the mainstay of Marc's business.

That was a huge blow to Marc. It destroyed a major portion of his business and a tremendous source of income. That was when he realized that specialization led to extinction, a principle he cites freely that is in keeping with his avocation, his attitude, and his business philosophy. Rather than closing his business, he adapted. He broadened the array of products that he sold; and he used his expertise, passion, and hard work ethic to shift his strategy. He became a breeder of magnificent, exotic birds and became so well known that he has developed a large export business selling his birds to aficionados in other countries.

You would think that his hard work

and determination would pay off, and it did for many years. Marc's first store was a 15- by 40-foot space; today he and his brood share a 15,000-square-foot facility. In addition to becoming a TV personality, he started a number of related businesses, including aquarium maintenance and dog grooming.

Enter another cruel twist of fate. A duck in New York State became ill with an influenza virus much feared in the Far East, where many of his exports find a home. Because of concerns about the virus, in June 2005, Japan issued a 6-month ban on the importing of birds from New York State. Although Marc's birds are well cared for and perfectly healthy, his exporting business has been shut down until the ban is lifted. Another big blow, and yet Marc is not bitter. "The world is constantly changing," he explains. "I have known that I wanted to work with animals ever since I was conscious. Bad things happen to good people all the time. You can't get angry. I have different things going on, and I can

always find a way to make more money.
I always look at the big picture."

Marc Morrone is an entrepreneur after
my own heart. He has thrived despite his
business setbacks by following the lead of
some early, intrepid Arctic pioneers. Marc
believes, "The most important thing in
business is to make as many friends as you
can. The Arctic explorers used to catch fish
as they traveled, and they would bury one in
the snow before they left camp. It was hard
to sacrifice that fish sometimes. But on the
way back, they could always count on having some food if they could make it to the
next camp. That is how I look at business.
You make as many friends as you can when
things are going well. You do things you
don't have to do in order to make friends. If
you run into some difficulty and have to
backtrack, they will be there, like the fish."
Marc's advice is sound. There are certain
things that just cannot be taken from you:
not by a change in government regulations,
not by a fire in the warehouse, not by a be-
trayal of a trustee, not even by a federal trial

and incarceration. The precious things that remain are your ideas, your determination, your work ethic, your loyal colleagues, your mentors, and all of the other friends who care about you and encourage you.

There is always value, even among the ashes

Several years ago, I was honored with an invitation to take part in a book project conceived by actress and author Marlo Thomas. Marlo, a former neighbor of mine in Westport, came up with the wonderful idea of asking 100 prominent people about the most valuable advice they received during a difficult period in their lives. The list included actors, politicians, businesspeople, sports stars, and other celebrities. Marlo explained that the proceeds from the book were to go to her favorite charity, St. Jude Children's Research Hospital, founded by her father, entertainer Danny Thomas. Her book was my favorite kind of Big Idea—it offered helpful, useful, and important advice that people need and want, and it was to contribute generously to a most worthy cause.

In her book, Marlo tells her own story of when she appeared as the lead in **Gigi,** her first big stage production, at Los Angeles's Laguna Playhouse. Thrilled as she was, Marlo experienced unfortunate treatment from reviewers and interviewers, who compared her endlessly to her father instead of focusing on her talents. She told her father she was so frustrated that she did not "want to be a Thomas anymore." He looked her in the eye and said that he had raised her to be a thoroughbred and that thoroughbreds run with blinders so they can keep their eyes focused straight ahead, with no distractions. "Don't listen to anyone comparing you to me or to anyone else. You just run your own race." The next night, there was a knock on her dressing room door, and a stage manager delivered a box holding an old pair of horse blinders and a note from her father reading, "Run your own race, Baby."

My contribution to the project was about a predicament I found myself in during my teenage years. My ninth-grade English teacher had assigned a book report, and I chose Nathaniel Hawthorne's **The Scarlet Letter.** This proved to be a very difficult novel for a naïve 13-year-old who had no idea what the word **adultery** meant. I turned to my father for some helpful advice and encouragement. He was, after all, very well read and an excellent writer. But my dad, with his strong work ethic, said, "Martha, you can do anything if you put your mind to it. Anything!" He carefully explained the definition of adultery, and I reread the book and completed my report.

To this day, I can still hear those wise words. You can come up with a Big Idea for something that millions of people need and want. You can become a self-made billionaire. You can refuse to cave in to detractors and manipulators despite enormous pressure. You can become friends with a fellow inmate and learn all about her life over a lunch of inedible prison food. You can emerge intact even through the toughest of times. **You can do anything!**

It is okay to overreact, but never panic

When building a business, you will face many challenges and find yourself in some very difficult situations. I cannot emphasize strongly enough that when this occurs, you cannot panic! Panic is a debilitating thing. Your heart races, your blood pressure rises, your breathing gets shallow, you may even feel ill. You revert to a primitive survival mode as your body sends adrenaline coursing through your veins and your brain stem tells you that you have two choices: flee or fight.

When something awful and unexpected occurs and threatens your business, I believe it is acceptable to overreact. You are the entrepreneur, the creator of a business that rides on your shoulders. When something negative is thrown your way, it is fine to let your staff know that you have intense feelings regarding the development. They will expect that from you and will actually want it from you. It is your business, your creation, after all, that has come under attack, and they are involved.

Panic, however, creates irrational behavior and actions that have not been well considered. These are often short-term solutions designed to make the pain stop, rather than thoughtful, strategic approaches that will actually help to solve the problem. When you sense danger approaching, go ahead and get upset, but do not do anything that cannot be undone. If I had panicked when I burnt my Moroccan b'steeya, I might have picked up the pigeon pies and thrown them away. By remaining calm and making good decisions, I was able to serve each guest at the Newmans' party a smaller sliver of a wonderfully unique dish. Not ideal, but hardly disastrous.

Take time to assess

When faced with a difficult challenge, remember the tools from Chapter 3—the telescope, the wide-angle lens, and the microscope. Using the microscope, examine up close what exactly has occurred. By looking closely at the details, you may find the problem is far smaller and less daunting. First assess what has happened very specifically and whether the situation demands immediate action.

Here is a scenario: Suppose you are a florist, and you arrive at your shop at 6:15 a.m. with a van full of fresh flowers that you just picked up from the wholesaler. On this particular Saturday, you have an order for two dozen arrangements—centerpieces that must be delivered for a wedding reception by 4 p.m. Your best floral designer was supposed to unlock your doors at 6 a.m. and meet you, ready to get to work. It surprises you that the shop is still closed. Once inside, you find your answering machine blinking. Your arranger's husband left a message saying his wife will not be in today because she has broken her wrist and is at the hospital.

You are in a difficult situation. There were only two of you scheduled in the shop today; she would have made the arrangements while you helped and served customers at the counter. You have two immediate problems: You have an excellent employee who has suffered a painful mishap. Your first call should be to put her at ease and wish her well. Your relationship is important. But, you also have two dozen centerpieces to compose to satisfy your customer. What do you do? You could close the shop and do the work yourself; you could call other employees for either a floral designer or a counter person to fill in; you could call another florist and either divide the work or subcontract him or her to do it; or you could alert your customer that you may not be able to deliver the order—hardly an option, in my opinion.

Grab the wide-angle lens. Look at the consequences of each choice. If you decide to protect your reputation by subcontracting out the job, how will the loss of those profits impact you? Should you lose a day's walk-in business so as not to disappoint the bride? How important is this order? How important is your walk-in business?

Next, peer through the telescope. What are the long-term implications of your options for solving this problem? Should you protect your good reputation at any cost? Can you form a backup relationship with another florist that could become a valuable partnership for the future?

Figure out what to cut and what to keep

When things are not looking so bright, sometimes the most difficult decision is knowing what to keep and what to cut, what to sell, what to discard. That is why a thorough assessment is so crucial. Look meticulously at your particular problem—is the thing really ruined or is it just damaged and still reparable? There is a big difference between the two. And stay focused on the core of your business—its heart and soul.

Let us revisit the flower shop. You have to consider the impact to your reputation if you disappoint a bride on her wedding day. She and her family will be furious, and rightly so. The damage to your business from a very public failure would far outweigh the impact of not opening your retail shop for one day. This little crisis may even help you realize that you can no longer run both a special order and a retail shop successfully at this stage of your business's life. Making the right decision requires evaluation, perhaps even advice from trusted mentors.

What if MSLO, during my troubles, had decided to change its name to something generic like Good Things Incorporated? What if they had purchased other businesses having nothing to do with our core competencies—a tropical resort, perhaps, or a shoe company—in order to diversify beyond the brand I had come to represent so personally? I can guarantee you that it would have been as nonsensical as if I had changed my name back to Martha Kostyra. My image and my name are intrinsically intertwined with the brand. What we did instead was to trust that our customers could separate my personal challenges from the brand's values. We continued to work hard to maintain the strength of the name that was the heart and soul of that brand.

This lesson is evident in the Gibson guitar example. When that company was faced with competition and other distractions, rather than cherishing and supporting their esteemed reputation, the management retreated to a low-price strategy. That proved to be the wrong choice. Restoring the company's reputation as a maker of high-quality guitars was the right choice. It is rarely ever the right choice to address a business problem by abandoning the thing that a company is known for.

There are, however, examples of companies that have changed their profile and even their products while staying true to the values customers associate with the brand. Abercrombie & Fitch is one such company. In 1892, the company known as Abercrombie & Fitch produced fabulous sportswear worthy of a weekend of foxhunting or shooting at the Windsors' estate. The store was frequented by worldly adventurers and explorers, and people from high society bought their jodhpurs and trekking apparel there. Unfortunately, the brand declined during the 1960s and 1970s, and the remaining stores closed their doors in 1976. The market for very-high-end sporting goods had given way to specialty retailers and to manufacturers who use high-tech, advanced materials. A newer and more successful company, The Limited, loved how the name, Abercrombie, rolls off the tongue and knew it still meant something to high-end clientele, so they purchased the brand. They repositioned it as a young adult label with very hip clothing styles and targeted customers who aspired to something more. The company went public in 1996, and since then the new Abercrombie has been embraced by a new generation as a trusted purveyor of young, contemporary classic sportswear.

When a Good Thing
masquerades as trouble

I want to share with you some insights from one of America's leading entrepreneurs, Steve Jobs, the founder of Apple Computer. Steve presented the commencement address at Stanford in 2005, and a friend kindly sent me the text. During his freshman year of college, he was confused and directionless. Feeling guilty about tuition costs, he thought it best to drop out. At age 20, Steve had a passion for computers, and he and his friend Steve Wozniak became classic garage inventors. Together they built Apple Computer, which grew at an astounding pace. Within 10 years, they had $2 billion in sales and 4,000 employees. In 1985 the company was doing very well on the strength of the Macintosh computer, which was a year old and really selling to consumers. "And then I got fired," he told the Stanford graduating class. "How can you get fired from a company you started?"

He explained that they had hired a soft-drink executive to run the business side of the company. At first, the executive and Steve got along quite well, until they had a major disagreement. Siding with the executive, the board of directors determined it would be best for the company to fire Steve. So there he was, 30 years old and fired from the company that had been his life for 10 years. "I was out. And very publicly out," he told the students. "What had been the focus of my entire adult life was gone, and it was devastating." You can imagine why his speech resonated with me.

Steve described the mourning period he went through, but he also told of a reawakening that led him to start his new computer company, NeXT, and then the extraordinary animation company Pixar. He also fell in love and got married. And then an uncanny thing happened—Apple bought NeXT. Suddenly, there was Steve, running Apple again. "I didn't see it then, but it turned out that getting fired from Apple was the best thing that could ever have happened to me."

A Martha by any other name . . .

I would like to add Steve Jobs's name to the list of entrepreneurs who believe that overcoming challenges not only builds character but often can lead to something better than that which existed before the problem ever appeared. At MSLO, despite my brief absence, we managed to plan and execute many exciting and wonderful new things—from my new television show in front of a live audience to **The Apprentice: Martha Stewart.** Great furniture was designed; housewares created; a newly acquired magazine, **Body+Soul**, was beautifully redesigned; and we planned the content for a 24-hour-a-day, 7-day-a-week satellite radio program on the Sirius radio station. Would we have done all these things were we not forced to step back and reevaluate who we were and where we wanted to go? Possibly not.

Call me Martha Kostyra or Martha Stewart or even call me M. Diddy. I have never been prouder of my company or looked to the future with more optimism.

Take risks,
not chances

Martha's Rule

IN BUSINESS, THERE'S A DIFFERENCE
BETWEEN A RISK AND A CHANCE. A WELL-
CALCULATED RISK MAY VERY WELL END UP
AS AN INVESTMENT IN YOUR BUSINESS. A
CARELESS CHANCE CAN CAUSE IT TO
CRUMBLE. AND WHEN AN OPPORTUNITY
PRESENTS ITSELF, NEVER ASSUME IT
WILL BE YOUR LAST.

NO ONE EVER SAID THAT STARTING a business was easy. If it were, more people would
do it. Likewise, no one ever said that **run-**

ning a business was easy. If that were true, most start-ups would succeed. But most fail. In an ideal business, one success would follow another, and the company would never falter. The reality is that companies, even the largest and most well known, falter not once, but many times.

Business is all about risk: assessing risk, managing risk. But it is also sometimes about taking a deep breath, looking all around you, then doing what my friend and colleague Mark Burnett calls "jumping in"— following a well-informed instinct or a calculated hunch even when others cannot see or understand your vision.

If you are starting or expanding a business, you may already realize that, like me, you, too, are a risk-taker. The natural question to ask yourself is whether what you are considering doing is a well-calculated risk or whether you are poised to take what I would call a chance—a long shot that depends largely on luck. I dislike taking chances; but I think taking a well-calculated risk is the cornerstone of entrepreneurship. I will tell you about several kinds of risks that I have

taken and introduce you to one of my favorite risk-takers.

The big financial bet

In business, your biggest risk is financial.
You may be presented with what feels like
the deal of a lifetime, but you must be fully
aware of all the details, the context, and the
timing before you can determine if the risk
is worth it. The same goes for hiring employees or considering a change of image for
your company. You must make a thorough
study to determine if such a change will
either pay off and help your business or cost
you dearly in the end.

Determining what is an acceptable risk
versus a long-shot chance is a dilemma for
all entrepreneurs. It's the kind of challenge
that wakes you up at 2 a.m. with a rapid,
pounding heartbeat. In the throes of weigh-
ing the risks of such a big decision, you'll
likely be nagged by such questions as: Why
aren't others doing this already? Am I ahead
of my time and right on, or is there a basic

flaw in my idea? Am I adding and subtracting the right numbers? Am I so smitten with the opportunity that I am rationalizing paying too much money for it? Or to put it more succinctly: Am I **crazy?**

The biggest financial risk I have ever taken was in 1997, when I borrowed $85 million and bought **Martha Stewart Living** from Time Warner. It turned out to be the best investment I have ever made. The media business is an exciting and risky one. A hot magazine, for example, attracts advertisers and readers and can generate very high profits in a short time if all goes well and all parts of the puzzle come together. But, as an old saying goes, the assets of a magazine walk out of the building every night and hail a cab or jump on the bus. Great employees make a magazine successful: talented editors, art directors, writers, stylists, photographers, and graphic artists. There are few tangible assets, and employees come and go, making it difficult to place a value on a publication when you are trying to buy or sell one.

In the late 1990s, we were a hot property;

but obviously $85 million sounded like a lot of money. My friends and advisors asked reasonable questions regarding the risk: What if the magazine's focus on the subject—living—goes out of style? What if key people leave? What if people just get tired of Martha Stewart?

Because the Martha Rules have been my credo all along, I had good answers to those questions. To begin, I understood my market far too well to believe that the interest in home could ever wane. In fact, I knew that all things related to house, garden, and family were just beginning a tremendous cycle of growth. Preparing food, eating, and entertaining are endlessly interesting topics. People are always looking for new ways to decorate and embellish their surroundings. We were staffed with talented, creative thinkers who wanted to make everyday living beautiful, practical, and invigorating to our readers. We would always adapt because we **were** our customers. I also was confident in my own commitment to this project.

By this time I had established myself as an expert in the broad category of homekeeping. I was a good cook, a good decorator, and a good gardener. My staff and I had created a large and growing library of real content—photographs, recipes, craft ideas, gardening advice, decorating tips, collecting information—all of "evergreen" value with a huge potential for synergy with other media platforms, such as television, radio, books, and newspaper columns. If we could combine all of those elements into one omni-media company, the whole of that would certainly be greater than the sum of its parts. This was not just about owning a business; it was about building a brand. I understood that we had our Big Idea.

The excitement of this idea was contagious, and the path was easy for me to see. Finding the $85 million, however, was not quite so easy. I first approached people who were used to taking big risks—investment bankers and venture capitalists—and quickly learned that, on Wall Street, the Golden Rule is turned on its head. Instead of "Do unto others as you would have them do unto you," the prevailing view is "He who has the gold makes the rule."

Investment bankers and venture capitalists are not averse to taking risks, but they often want to be compensated for it at a cost that is, frankly, staggering. I met with one venture capitalist who told me he would gladly fund the deal for a 70/30 split of the ownership, which I assumed meant I would take 70 percent and he would take 30 percent. To me, that seemed like an awfully high percentage for him to receive, but at least it sounded better than the deal proposed by a different venture capitalist who demanded 50 percent. You can imagine my shock when the second fellow clarified that he would be the one to take the 70 percent! I left **that** meeting quickly.

Still, I was determined to put this plan in motion, and I explored every possible option. Finally, I decided that I would borrow the money from a bank, using my personal net worth as collateral along with the newly negotiated contracts I had with Kmart and other strategic partners. My attorneys at the time reviewed the plan, and they advised me not to personally sign for that amount of money and to take a much more conservative approach. They said I was being foolhardy—in other words, crazy. They said I was taking too big of a chance.

The lawyers were not alone in their thinking. Others close to me expressed similar concerns. I was, after all, exploring uncharted territory, but I saw it as being entirely navigable. My vision was broader than simply buying and controlling my magazine. The purchase would provide a platform from which the company could grow in many different directions, offering useful and necessary information and wonderful products to our valued customers. I knew that although it had never been done, that didn't mean it couldn't be done.

We had other major concerns during the early years of ownership of the company. At the start of my daily television show, some people warned me that my growing television popularity would detract from my magazine audience. Why would people buy the magazine when they could watch me on television for free? But my instincts told me I was connecting with my customers. I knew readers would become viewers and viewers would become readers because the two media are complementary. Needless to say, I carried out my plan and bought the company from Time Inc. The business continued to prosper and expand, new initiatives were explored, a strategy was formalized, and 2 years later the company went public. I paid back all my debts and obligations, the company's value soared, and I became a billionaire overnight. In my experience, being "crazy" has really paid off.

Analyzing everyday risks

It may be awhile before you have to decide whether to take a risk as big as borrowing $85 million, but there is a good lesson here. It involves an old expression that chance favors the prepared mind. If you have laid the essential groundwork and followed my previous rules, you should find the confidence to separate reasonable risk from careless chance, and you will have the good sense to thoroughly analyze opportunities from every possible relevant angle. Should I sign a long-term lease or a short-term lease? Should I hire employees or use contractors and consultants? Should I borrow money from friends and family or take on a business partner? Should I develop and train an employee, knowing she may leave me at any time? Some of these decisions may seem rather mundane, and the right decision will not necessarily pave your path to fame and fortune; but the wrong decision can be so costly that it can put you out of business.

One of an entrepreneur's most basic decisions is the "make versus buy" decision. For example, you may be a general contractor who is also skilled at tile setting. Your ability to do your own tile work has been a source of excellent profits in your construction and renovation projects. But as your business grows, hiring an outside tile setter or doing it yourself on any given job begins to involve a risk calculation. You must weigh how quickly the job needs to be done and whether your time is more profitably spent managing other people on this and other jobs. You must also analyze the subcontractor options you have. If the only outside tile setter available is both expensive and incapable of the quality you demand, you will have to find the time to do the job yourself so that you do not both risk your reputation and eliminate your profit margin. As you can see, there are risks to both options, so you must sit down and thoroughly think through the consequences of each.

MSLO faced an exciting make-versus-buy decision recently. We realized that the self-care market was ripe for a quality magazine, but the subject matter and advertising market were just enough beyond our core expertise that we were not entirely comfortable starting a magazine from scratch, as we had done with **Everyday Food.**

Everyday Food was a "make" decision. It was an idea I had been mulling over for a number of years. It was fun and exciting to see people who had been working in one format—the large, luxurious format of **Martha Stewart Living**—embrace the challenge of designing a completely different kind of magazine. We had the resources at hand. We had chefs, test kitchens, art directors, and highly skilled photographers ready to explore, create, and build a new property.

Many of us in the company felt that a magazine combining care of the body and mind, nutrition, exercise, and alternative medicine was compelling and exciting. We found ourselves increasingly interested in subjects such as yoga and massage, herbal remedies, stress-relief solutions, and helpful strategies for making major life decisions or simplifying one's routine to create more time for leisure or family activities. We had already been thinking about incorporating some of this subject matter into our existing magazines, although it really did not fit well in our formats. Then the perfect opportunity came along. In 2004, the owners of **Body+Soul** offered to sell the magazine to us.

The price was attractive, but it required a very thoughtful risk analysis of this opportunity. On the risk side of the ledger was the fact that we had never purchased a magazine before, never adapted other peoples' ideas and concepts in such a "store-bought" way. Additionally, **Body+Soul** was located in Boston, and we were in Manhattan. Would that make things too complicated? **Body+Soul** had a very good staff, but it needed to revamp the art direction and increase staffing and budgets. Could we find the right people to accomplish those key elements? Another important calculation was that this magazine was not about style, taste, or preference, but about expert advice in matters of health, body care, and nutrition. Did the magazine have the right bylines and the right experts to satisfy our target customer audience?

We found that there is a lot of activity in the self-care area, but it is still considered very much a niche market in publishing. We also discovered that there are a number of narrow-scope magazines published that focus on individual aspects of these topics, such as yoga, alternative medicine, and simplifying life. Within a growing market, it is important to stake out an early position, but if you get in too early, you have to invest heavily in building circulation and brand, and that can be costly.

As we made our study, we looked at our own in-house resources to see if it would make more sense for us to create our own magazine. As with **Everyday Food,** we would be spending money up front to design and staff a brand-new magazine; then we would have to build a subscriber base and an advertising base. In such a niche market, that was somewhat daunting. It seemed a better idea to take advantage of **Body+Soul**'s 230,000 subscribers and make them even happier with a freshly redesigned magazine, building up from there rather than attempting to slice the self-care market pie into yet another wedge and to win the established audience base over to a brand-new magazine. Having the existing customer base is what finally convinced us to make the deal to buy **Body+Soul,** lock, stock, and barrel.

As you can see, this was not an easy or "just follow your intuitions" type of decision. You can follow your instincts if you weigh your options first—after analysis, discussion, research, and input from your team. Fortunately, the price of **Body+Soul** was reasonable, and the project also served as a good laboratory for us to see how we would handle diversification into a new area, with a new brand, and a remote operation. So far, it looks like we made a very good decision. In a short period of time circulation has grown by 80,000 subscribers, the look of the magazine is steadily improving, and the category is strengthening. We took a calculated risk that we could improve upon someone else's ideas, and it is working! And we took a calculated risk that we could give a remote team the freedom to be creative experts while offering the guidance for quality that we are famous for in all of our media platforms. I think the acquisition of **Body+Soul** will turn out to be quite a Good Thing.

Was I prepared to trump Trump?

The entertainment business is full of risk-loving entrepreneurs. People do not necessarily think of actors, directors, or producers as entrepreneurs, but they are. They come up with a Big Idea, develop it, invest in it, nurture it, and try to sell it to the public. When it works, they can enjoy huge financial success and acclaim. When it does not work, some disappear into obscurity. And so my decision to work with Mark Burnett on **The Apprentice: Martha Stewart** and on a new live-audience format for my daily daytime television show, **Martha,** represented a well-calculated but big and deeply personal risk for both me and the company. It also involved some risk for Mark. In fact, I know there are people who, when they first heard that I had agreed to do **The Apprentice,** were scratching their heads in pure bewilderment. And there were others who just murmured, "Smart."

MARK BURNETT
"Jump in"

As the producer of **Eco-Challenge, Survivor, The Apprentice, The Contender,** and **Rock Star,** Mark Burnett is given credit for revolutionizing television. He has been called the young Father of Reality TV, has won an Emmy award, and was named as one of the Top 101 Most Powerful People in Entertainment by **Entertainment Weekly.** Not bad for a former British paratrooper who arrived in this country with $600 and no college education, and whose resumé listed a nanny, insurance salesman, and T-shirt salesperson at California's Venice Beach as credentials while he looked for a job in television.

Like all good entrepreneurs, Mark has overcome numerous stumbling blocks. For example, when he pitched his idea for **Survivor,** the first couple of networks looked at him strangely and turned him down. But his idea has been proven so dramatically right that Mark now has the confidence, and funding, to try all kinds of innovative things, including a collaboration with me.

During my legal travails, but before my trial in 2004, I received a call from a very good friend in Los Angeles. She had been speaking to Mark, and he expressed interest in meeting me. To be honest, I was intrigued, so I agreed, and he flew to New York. I liked him instantly, and he felt the same about me. I found him good-natured, optimistic, incisive, decisive, and straightforward. Although he was deeply concerned about my legal affairs, he was not put off by them. He explained that he watched my television show with great interest and he was looking for a successful businesswoman to extend **The Apprentice** format. It was a very good meeting. I later invited Mark and his girlfriend, the lovely actress Roma Downey, to Skylands, my house in Maine. Over that weekend, I discovered that he also was fun, smart, and very good company. I knew I could work with him.

Since this chapter is about risk, I'll tell you about his attitude toward the subject. Mark has authored a book called **Jump In! Even If You Don't Know How to Swim.** In it he describes hair-raising encounters with lethal snakes and monsoons, natural challenges he faced when he was making shows like **Sur-**

vivor and **Eco-Challenge.** Reading the book, you understand that he is a hard-working, adventure-loving person who is not afraid to follow his hunches. "I operate on instinct," he says.

While that may be true, Mark has made himself an expert in his brand of television, and he spares no expense and no effort to bring the highest quality values to his shows that he possibly can. That is what I found so appealing. We are both risk-takers, but he and I are different in some fundamental ways. I doubt I would ever just "jump in" if I could not swim, but I might if I had read a book on how to swim. Mark would follow his instincts, jump in, and figure out then how to swim; and he behaves in the same way when he explores ideas and picks projects. He also does extensive research to be certain he can follow through on an idea in the best possible way, in the way that he consults a map and compass when he's off on some amazing adventure. "You have to focus on every day's actions and what the consequences of those actions are," says Mark. "You must pay attention to every step and keep checking to make sure you are still on course. Stupid people decide to take a risk, and then they don't pay attention. They just keep blindly heading in the original direction."

You might think that I would have bristled at the idea of hosting **The Apprentice.** My edition was to be a sequel of sorts to the original and popular show that starred Donald Trump. I have never played second fiddle. MSLO specializes in creating and originating ideas. I thought that my friend Donald had done a very nice job on his version of **The Apprentice.** Did the world want or even need another version of this reality show? Did I really want to follow someone else's act? And what about creative control? We had never given that to anyone before. Could we trust Mark's standards? Would his standards equal mine? Would his way of doing things show off my company at its very best?

But remember what I said about change:

When you're through changing, you're through. I liked and respected Mark Burnett immediately. In trying to convince me to do **The Apprentice,** he made me his customer, and he connected with me. When I was in Alderson, he visited me several times. In our conversations, he inspired me to think about all kinds of new things we could try on my new live show, and I agreed to let him serve as my executive producer. He had convinced me that he was, indeed, an expert in this form of television, that his work ethic was excellent, and that his instincts were sharp. He also seemed to understand the big picture of my company's story while so many others were focusing on the short-term details. "People told me it was a risk to work with Martha," Mark has said. "I could see that her brand was way more full of integrity and future value than anyone was giving the company credit for. I looked at the situation and said, 'This will pass.'"

Working with Mark involved some interesting image decisions for me, as well. For one thing, we talked about showing more of my personality than I have revealed in the past on my television shows, in part because Mark spent many hours studying tapes of me and said he thought I seemed much more at ease when I was a guest on other peoples' shows, like with David Letterman, Jay Leno, and Conan O'Brien. Here are a few more tidbits that he noticed about me: I like a good laugh. I love a good practical joke. I like to goof around a bit. Would it hurt to show that side of me? Mark and I took a well-calculated risk that a new, more spontaneous format with a live audience was a wonderful way for me to come back from my difficult experiences.

When it came to the making of **The Apprentice: Martha Stewart,** I could really see the wisdom of doing this program. As I focused on the show, I realized it provided us with a different sort of platform to display the excellence of the company, its philosophy, its beliefs, and its commitment to Good Things. Clearly, we have created an original, fabulous, very American company within the American dream. I am so pleased that I took the risk, that Mark was wise enough to take this risk, and that we embarked on this television adventure together. Mark has a favorite North African proverb that he repeats to would-be entrepreneurs who would like to follow in his footsteps. He tells them, "Choose your companions before you choose your road."

That "opportunity of a lifetime" will not be your last

What if I had not taken the risk and had said no to Mark Burnett? I know the answer to such a question. I would be doing something else interesting, something else of high quality and uniquely fitting to celebrate my return to television. I have observed that inexperienced businesspeople sometimes make poor decisions because they are terrified that opportunity will pass them by and they will regret it for the rest of their lives. That is rarely, if ever, true.

Warren Buffett, the brilliant and amazingly successful investor, often repeats a valuable piece of advice about investing that also applies to business opportunities. He uses the following baseball analogy: "There are no called strikes in investing." Simply stated, even if you let a terrific opportunity pass you by, you will never be called out of the game.

You should never try something that makes you uncomfortable or that you are ill prepared to undertake just because you think you may never get another chance. That chance will come. Prepare yourself mentally, emotionally, and intellectually first, and you will be able to differentiate a long shot from a good, well-calculated risk. You will also become more aware that the world is full of interesting opportunities. Taking risks can make anyone feel uneasy, but if you are feeling deeply worried and have strong misgivings about an opportunity, let it go. Another chance will surely come your way.

It is hardly a secret that I am a collector and an accumulator of many things, from fine antiques to kitchen kitsch. I love the histories of my collections—the various materials used and why, the fine distinctions, and what makes one piece rarer than another. Because I am so tuned into my collections, I can recall, with dismay, every object I have seen, fallen in love with, and allowed to slip by. I close my eyes and can visualize exactly that stack of Spode Blackbird dishes that I allowed to go to a higher bidder at a little auction on the Hudson River 41 years ago. It pains me that I did not acquire a gorgeous piece of American furniture called a "chest on legs" at another auction in Worthington, Massachusetts, in 1966. And more recently, I am still irked that I refused to purchase an incredible Roman bronze from 100 AD that was offered to me by a Swiss art dealer in 2000. I procrastinated, lost the opportunity, and I am very sorry that I did. It will probably never come on the market again in my lifetime, but if it does, I will be there with my checkbook in hand.

Ask me about missed investment opportunities or business deals I wish I had made, though, and I can honestly tell you that I hardly remember them. Throughout the years, many people have brought us some interesting business proposals. We invested in some of these and rejected many more. The reason they have vanished from my recollection is that there was nothing unusual or rare about them. We are a nation of wonderful, creative, and innovative people, and new opportunities are always emerging. You are never out of the game simply because you did not take a given risk or a given job or did not buy a given company when it was available. Keep in mind, as you assess your options, that business opportunities are not like rare objects attained for a private collection. They are dynamic, flexible, and malleable entities that come and go and change and can be adapted to the times. Never dwell upon the ideas you did not seize. Instead, place your energy into being alert for the next opportunity.

If the word *risk* makes you nervous, call it an investment

For me, a well-calculated business risk is an investment you make in yourself and in your employees. A careless chance, on the other hand, would be if you suddenly agreed to merge your company with the company of someone you have been seated next to on a cross-country flight, who may have impressed you in some particular way. A well-calculated risk involves investigating the deal, having your staff analyze the numbers, spending time with the potential partner to understand his or her style and the value of his or her business. Only then can you decide if it is a smart investment.

When you are planning a business or to expand your business, it is often difficult deciding what kinds of investments you should be making. Here are some guidelines.

First, invest in yourself. Invest in exploring all the details of your passion, then turn yourself into an expert. Once you feel like an expert, do not spend too much time partaking of your passion. You may find it exciting and enjoyable, but the time spent is not free and not without risk. You must see your path. You must devote the necessary time and resources to further your education, whether formal or informal. Bill Gates took a big risk by investing in his vision and dropping out of Harvard in his freshman year to realize his dream. On the other hand, Susan Hanneman took a calculated risk by quitting her job with us as an editor to return to school for her MBA so that she could venture further in her career as a food professional. Those were two good choices. Obviously, everyone's situation is different, unique, and challenging.

When I envisioned creating my book **Entertaining,** I learned as much as I could about food photography, book design, typography, and food styling. If I had listened to the many negative comments regarding the making of such a book, the project would never have gotten off the ground. I knew what I wanted and how I wanted it to look. I was not a professional photographer, but I studied how different cameras functioned, what kinds of pictures they took, and the different lighting techniques that would make the photos look the most appetizing for the book I envisioned. I pored over photography books and art books to learn how to present images in a compelling way. I understood that to achieve my goal, I truly had to learn as much as I could about these skills and techniques. I could not and would not fake such knowledge.

This was a critical component of the talk I gave about business to the inmates at Alderson. I told them to start out by believing in themselves. Know that you are strong, smart, and you can do anything you put your mind to. Once you realize that and you have identified a passion, invest in yourself. Figure out what you need to know, what kind of experience and expertise you need to develop to do the things that you feel in your heart you will enjoy and that will sustain you both mentally and economically. You are not biding your time or enduring a course—you are investing in your own future. That future will be more fruitful and satisfying because of the well-calculated risk that you are taking today. If you have followed your passion and pursued a career in a milieu you love—it will not feel like work!

I think back to all the fun I had years ago, during my modeling days. I enjoyed posing for photographers, but how could I ever have imagined that the confidence I gained back then in front of the camera would be beneficial in my business so many years later? Similarly, I am reminded of another thing that Steve Jobs mentioned in his speech at Stanford University. He told the graduates that after he dropped out of college, he became very interested in calligraphy and took a class so he could learn it. He was fascinated because it was such a beautiful form of penmanship. Today, he credits that interest in calligraphy as the reason why he made certain that Macintosh computers feature such beautiful typography, setting them apart from other brands of computers.

Second, after you invest in your personal education and are trying to determine what to invest in next, take out your telescope. Focus on what your long-term goals are, and make investments that will enable you to achieve those goals, even if they involve short-term sacrifices.

For example, to become an architect, one must spend many years in training and in low-paying apprenticeships before one can design a single building of one's own. And cities like New York and Los Angeles are brimming with aspiring actors, working in restaurants and sharing apartments so they can afford acting classes and have their days free to attend auditions. They are all in pursuit of the big, life-changing break; and the thought of it is so exciting, short-term sacrifices seem well worth it.

On the road to becoming an entrepreneur, there typically comes a time when you figure out where you want to go. You take a hard look at what it will take to get there, and you embark on a journey that, in the beginning, feels much more like a student's budget tour of Europe than a first-class trip on the Orient Express. In 1990, when I convinced Time Warner to publish my first magazine, **Martha Stewart Living,** the company graciously gave us what I suspect was the absolute worst office space in the entire Time-Life building in midtown Manhattan. One thing that I found amusing about the magazine business was that, for all the beautiful photography and luxurious, airy layout spreads, the companies that produce much of that beauty are so often run out of cramped, drab cubicles bursting with messy stacks of books, newspapers, catalogs, photographs, press materials, reporter notes, and layouts taped to the walls.

In those early days, when we were trying to prove ourselves, I spent many hours with Gael Towey and my first editor, Isolde Motley, tripping over each other in our crowded, hot, airless suite of rooms in the Time-Life building. The offices were on a high floor directly above the heating and ventilation equipment floor. Our offices vibrated, and the equipment right below us literally heated the floor. I still recall my feet being swollen whenever I had spent a long day in the office!

Yet, I recall those exciting days fondly. We were trying to prove something—to our parent publisher, to ourselves, to the world. We were enthusiastic, energetic entrepreneurs, and we were not about to let a little thing like tiny offices or even swollen feet get in the way of the dream. We were frugal about absolutely everything that did not involve the quality of the product. We did not complain about the accommodations because we were trying to convince our publisher to spend more money on better photographers and graphic designers. Those were the things that were so important to building what we were trying to achieve. We took a well-calculated risk that by sacrificing some personal comforts in the short term, we would build something of lasting value that would reward us personally and professionally many times over. And that is exactly what happened. The same can happen to you if you invest wisely in yourself.

Make it beautiful

Martha's Rule 10

LISTEN INTENTLY, LEARN NEW THINGS
EVERY DAY, BE WILLING TO INNOVATE, AND
BECOME AN AUTHORITY YOUR CUSTOMERS
WILL TRUST. AS AN ENTREPRENEUR, YOU
WILL FIND GREAT JOY AND SATISFACTION IN
MAKING YOUR CUSTOMERS' LIVES EASIER,
MORE MEANINGFUL, AND MORE BEAUTIFUL.

I BELIEVE THAT THE BEST WAY to be organized and productive is to follow a list, and
I try to make one for myself every morning.
Always at the top of my list is to make life
better. I am always asking myself how I can
improve the lives of my customers, my col-

leagues, my shareholders, my family, and my friends. Making their lives better is important to me; and in doing so, I feel that my life is better.

The wonderful letter you will read below was sent to me in the midst of my legal troubles. It was a period of great stress and distraction for me, but reading Paulette's note made me forget my problems for just a while and allowed me to focus on that priority of mine—the heart and soul of my business, a business built around my views about the importance of the home, the nobility of the homemaker, and the joy that comes from simple, pleasurable activities such as watching birds or planting and harvesting heirloom tomatoes.

May 13, 2004

Dear Martha,

I've just finished my daily walk. I'm up to 75 minutes! I decided to take a break before going into the kitchen to bake cornbread to go with the chili we're having for lunch. From

my computer, I can look out over our garden. It's finally taking shape. The trees no longer look like they were planted yesterday. There's a wren building in one of our birdhouses. Yesterday I counted 10 different kinds of birds at our feeders in a 20-minute time period. I've seen over 48 different kinds of birds in our yard, including an illusive rose-breasted nuthatch and a peregrine falcon. Fortunately for the nuthatch, he wasn't in the yard when the falcon arrived. I'm looking at putting in bamboo flooring. I've heard it's environmentally friendly and harder than oak or maple.

I did none of those things before I discovered your magazine and television show. You see, many years back, I quit my job at a theological library. I realized I had learned as much as I could there. It was time to move onto something new. The smart thing would have been looking for another job before quitting, but I wasn't and didn't. So there I sat in an empty house, wondering what the heck to do. My friends wondered what was up. I was asked if I was just sitting around the house all day and eating bonbons. I denied it. Technically, I wasn't lying. I was munching on mixed nuts and seedless grapes, and I occasionally sat around outside.

But I still was clueless what to do next. So I turned on the idiot box and started to watch a lot of the idiot stuff that comes on the airwaves during that wasteland called daytime television. During my mindless channel surfing, I happened upon a half-hour show. It immediately caught my attention since the woman on it was making sense and was telling me something I wanted to know, something I wanted to learn. I was hooked. Every day, I took a break from doing basically nothing to watch someone who was doing something worthwhile. That woman doing something worthwhile was you.

With each passing day, I gradually got out of my funk and started my new life. I tried your recipes, repainted my rooms, and planted six different varieties of tomatoes in my garden. My husband and I tasted them, and we're unable to pick our favorite. We narrowed it down to Brandywine and Mortgage Lifter.

I guess I owe a lot to you and your staff—beautiful gardens, homemade bread, ideas on remodeling our home, and yes, my future. You see, during the time I spent reading your magazine, watching your show, and working on projects they inspired, I found out what to do with my life. Later this afternoon, I will sit down and do it. I will work on the third draft of my book. My editor tells me that it's not unusual to have to do a few rewrites on a first novel.

Martha, no matter what the future may bring, remember you have changed people's lives for the better. I look forward to reading future edi-

tions of your magazine. Oh, I've got to go! Your show's coming on. Ask anyone, I never miss it. Not even for you, Martha.

> **Sincerely,**
> **Paulette Myers**
> **Dubuque, IA**

When I read such letters, they reinforce my vision. They remind me to keep our standards high and our quality impeccable so that others, like Paulette, can rise above the "idiot" chatter, as she puts it, and make their lives more beautiful, as well.

"Make it beautiful" is a mantra that I repeat several times each day. I say it to my editors as they prepare a layout for the magazine. I say it to my art directors as we stand at the viewing wall and try to pick the "just right" image for the covers of our magazines. I say it to the chefs in the test kitchen creating new recipes. I say it to the stylists who are propping a room for a decorating story. I say it to my lighting director on the television set as we prepare to shoot a show. And I say it every time I meet with the design teams who create the thousands of products we sell: "Is that a coffee cup that will make you happy? Is that a design that you will want to buy for your kitchen or your home? Is that a sheet that you would want on your bed or on your child's bed? Do you think it is beautiful?" If the answer is no or a wavering maybe, the product should not be manufactured, it should not leave the design table, it has no place in our customers' lives.

"Make it beautiful." It is something everyone should say, no matter what the product, the plan, the project. It should be a phrase that every entrepreneur remembers and repeats.

Within these pages I have introduced you to wonderful entrepreneurs who have made their customers' worlds more beautiful in some way. Marc Morrone offers the beauty of his glorious, pampered pets and his vast knowledge of them. Because of Airborne, customers of Victoria Knight-McDowell can breathe in the beautiful aromas of roses, pine trees, and fresh-baked breads because they are not stuffed up with the common cold. Dr. Brent Ridge wants to be certain that his patients can hear beautiful musical compositions and not suffer as poor Beethoven did. And Eva Scrivo makes her customers feel beautiful both in the mirror and within because of the nurturing they receive in her salon.

I reflect fondly on those visionary entrepreneurs who have inspired me personally: Julia Child, Bill Gates, Steve Jobs, Estée Lauder, Larry Page, Walt Disney, Henry Ford, Pierre Omidyar, Sergey Brin, and Ralph Lauren. I hope that from my advice and encouragement, you, too, will find inspiration. I hope you will seek out caring and generous mentors of your own who can help you navigate the difficult currents of your business while reminding you how much fun and how exciting it all really is.

Ultimately, however, as an entrepreneur, I predict that your greatest joys will come from knowing that you are doing something good, something worthwhile, something useful and practical, something valuable—and something beautiful. You will care about quality in a world where quality is often declining. You will listen to your customers in a world where that business value is often ignored. You will be a respected expert in a world that is overflowing with information but deficient in reliable sources of the "best" advice. You are going to feel the energy that comes from pursuing your passion, and you are going to find yourself having trouble separating your work life from your personal life because you enjoy your work so much.

It gives me great pride to consider the mountain of beautiful images and ideas and products that my business has brought to our readers, viewers, and customers. For us, homekeeping is an art and also a celebration of life—of family, friends, traditions, good food, and creativity. The home should be a place to cherish, a place to find comfort, and yes, a place to find beauty.

No matter what your Big Idea may be, no matter what you feel passionate about, no matter what business you are in or about to enter, follow my rules and you should realize success. And last, but far from least, remember to **make it beautiful!**

Index

G

Gates, Bill, 24, 34–35, 301–2, 315

General Electric, 125–26

Gibson guitar company, 194–97, 270

Glassybaby, 54–55, 143

Goals, 304–5

Good Thing origin of, 14–15 examples of, 179

Graham, Bette Nesmith, 46

Graham, Katharine, 24

H

Hanneman, Susan, 239–42, 302

Heronswood Nursery, 17–20

Hewlett, Bill, 60

Hewlett-Packard, 60

Hinkley, Dan, 17–20, 21, 33, 63, 171

Hiring strategies, 224–31. **See also** Employees

HomeGrocer.com, 62–63

Hoverson, Joelle, 83–87, 91, 162, 171, 222

I

Ideas. **See** Big Ideas

Image, 142

Information, offering free to customers, 117–21

Innovation, 191–92

Insurance, 90, 94–96

Internet. **See also** Web site to listen to customers, 108 to promote business, 171–73

Investment bankers, 280–81

ABOUT MARTHA STEWART

Time magazine has recognized Martha Stewart as one of America's 25 Most Influential People. **Fortune** magazine has called her one of the 50 Most Powerful Women in American Business. She has appeared on the list of New York's 100 Most Influential Women in Business, in **Crain's New York Business.** And she has been named to the Forbes 400.

In her award-winning magazine, **Martha Stewart Living**; on her daytime syndicated show, **Martha**; in her programming on Sirius satellite radio; and in her best-selling product lines, Martha shares the creative principles and practical ideas that have made her America's most trusted guide to stylish living. She has been awarded numerous honors and distinctions from the worlds of business, education, television, media, culinary arts, and retail. She is the host of the NBC-TV reality show **The Apprentice: Martha Stewart** and the founder of Martha Stewart Living Omnimedia, Inc.